THE Portable Dissertation Advisor

THE Portable Dissertation Advisor

Miles T. Bryant

CORWIN PRESS
A Sage Publications Company
Thousand Oaks, California

For information:

Corwin Press
A Sage Publications Company
2455 Teller Road
Thousand Oaks, California 91320
www.corwinpress.com

Sage Publications Ltd.
6 Bonhill Street
London EC2A 4PU
United Kingdom

Sage Publications India Pvt. Ltd.
B-42, Panchsheel Enclave
Post Box 4109
New Delhi 110 017 India

Printed in the United States of America

Library of Congress Cataloging-in-Publication Data

Bryant, Miles Taft.
The portable dissertation advisor / Miles T. Bryant.
    p. cm.
Includes bibliographical references and index.
ISBN 0-7619-4695-0 (cloth) — ISBN 0-7619-4696-9 (pbk.)
    1. Doctor of education degree. 2. Dissertations, Academic-Handbooks, manuals, etc.
3. Report writing-Handbooks, manuals, etc. I. Title.
LB1742.B79 2004
378.2'42—dc22

                                        2003016033

This book is printed on acid-free paper.

03   04   05   06   10   9   8   7   6   5   4   3   2   1

Acquisitions Editor:	Rachel Livsey
Editorial Assistant:	Phyllis Cappello
Production Editor:	Kristen Gibson
Copy Editor:	Toni Williams
Typesetter:	C&M Digitals (P) Ltd.
Cover Designer:	Tracy E. Miller
Indexer:	Sheila Bodell
Graphic Designer:	Lisa Miller

Contents

Preface

I hope that this book will live up to its title as a portable advisor. The book is directed at those unable to work as full-time students on a university campus or who must study from a distance. Throughout this book, I refer to such graduate students as nontraditional graduate students. Often the nontraditional student does not have ready access to information about the doctoral dissertation. She or he will not have the information-laden informal networks available to the full-time, on-campus student. Lacking quick access to a research library, the nontraditional student may have difficulty identifying relevant research. Communicating with an advisor and the members of a supervisory committee may prove to be a daunting task. The pace of the academic calendar may be at odds with the work-life of the nontraditional student. In short, there are many reasons why the nontraditional student operates at a disadvantage. This book is intended to offset this disadvantage.

The dissertation phase of doctoral study is one full of myth and convention at most institutions. This book also attempts to dispel myth and reveal convention. I want to say at the outset that each person's journey through the dissertation is unique. Paradoxically, your study will look like no other person's study, and your study will also look like all other dissertations. By this I mean that when you have completed your study, you will have made decisions appropriate to your exploration, but you will also have made these decisions in light of those requirements that faculty members impose on your study. Hence your study will be like no other, but it will share common characteristics with the conventions of the doctoral dissertation.

The dissertation phase of one's doctoral program is potentially a phase of great satisfaction and accomplishment, metaphorically like climbing a challenging mountain. Effort, labor, risk, new insights, and satisfaction are all associated with the task. For some, the most rewarding aspect of the mountain is the climb to the top. For others, the reward comes by reaching the top. We experience and value the journey differently. There is a key difference, however, between climbing a mountain and writing a dissertation. Mountain climbers have noted that one may climb a mountain because it is there. One does not usually write a dissertation because it is there. One writes a dissertation in large part because one is required to write a dissertation. One may eagerly carry out a study and report findings, but one does not usually leap to carry out a study under the supervision and critical eyes of an advisor and of a group of university professors. It is a challenge to find a topic; it is a greater challenge to find a topic acceptable to the supervisory committee; it is an even greater challenge to implement a study that will also be acceptable. But, that is the goal.

You, the doctoral student, will appreciate this challenge more fully on the day when you shake your advisor's hand and are complimented with the title of doctor before your name.

Most doctoral program faculty supervisors require a proposal or preproposal prior to the final determination of the dissertation study. This book should be helpful company in that regard as well. Structured opportunities to have one's ideas discussed and criticized almost always help students develop dissertations. For the traditional on-campus student, such conversations occur with peers and with one's advisor. For the nontraditional student, such opportunities for interaction are different. This book provides many suggestions for interacting with others.

The book is not intended to stand in place of the advisor; rather, the book is intended to stand with the advisor as an additional resource for you. As I will say repeatedly, consistent communication with an advisor is one of the factors associated with successful completion of the dissertation. If you are a nontraditional student unfamiliar with the U.S. approach to doctoral education, you should realize that U.S. and European universities differ in their approach to doctoral education. In the U.S. university, the advisor usually plays a significant role in the development of the dissertation proposal and monitors the dissertation process from start to finish.

I should like to add a note for doctoral student advisors, particularly in the various education disciplines. In recent years, many of us have experienced changes in our work with doctoral students. It has become more common for the student to select a dissertation topic that may lie outside our areas of expertise and interest. The part-time doctoral student is more common. And the student who must work full time while writing the dissertation is also more common. Thus the generative conversations that used to characterize the relationship of advisor and student are less likely to occur. This changing relationship may not be desirable but it is, nonetheless, a reality. For all these reasons, a book such as this should help ease your difficulties in working with a nontraditional student. I wish also to note that as this book has circulated in draft form, many doctoral students have told me it would have been helpful for them to have a copy of it as they began their doctoral program, long before they actually began to work on the dissertation.

There are a number of examples in this book drawn from dissertation studies. Many of these are taken from work completed or undertaken at the University of Nebraska—Lincoln because my most sustained contact with doctoral students has taken place at that institution. These examples should not be dismissed as nonrepresentative because they were written at one institution. A perusal of dissertation abstracts reveals a commonality of conventions in doctoral-degree-granting institutions and a similarity in the types of work done by doctoral students. While our practices in guiding doctoral students through the dissertation may vary, our end products display a similarity.

My perspective on the doctoral dissertation is intentionally pragmatic in large part because I have found over many years of helping students construct dissertations that doctoral students want pragmatic advice. To be sure, there are intrinsic reasons for doctoral research; to be sure, there are weighty intellectual issues to be examined; to be sure, getting the degree may not always be seen as the most important motivation for completing the dissertation. Still, there is the matter of "getting done." This book is intended to help.

Chapter 1 presents what I call first steps. The sections in this chapter cover a range of issues and topics that doctoral students typically experience as they begin to define both their topic of study and the framework within which they intend to carry out the study. Chapter 2 covers the introductory chapter of the dissertation or dissertation proposal. I include in this section the typical material that the advisor and supervisory committee expect in the introductory section of the dissertation. Chapter 3 covers the literature review and includes information about using the research library. Chapter 4 identifies the general issues associated with the research method and identifies some problem areas that doctoral students often experience as they seek to design a method to answer their research questions. In Chapters 5 and 6, I go over issues associated with reporting the data that have been gathered and in writing up results. The last chapter, Chapter 7, discusses a number of topics that frequently surface as doctoral students seek to better understand events like the oral defense, dissertation abstracts, the supervisory committee, and graduation. Four appendices provide additional resources: (a) an annotated bibliography, (b) a bibliography of helpful dissertations, (c) an assessment form for evaluating the dissertation proposal, and (d) a list of suggested activities for a dissertation support group.

You will note many little quotations with which I begin sections. Implicit in these quotes is some message or bit of humor that I would convey to you about the section. I also wish to model for you the rhetorical device of beginning a piece of writing with a quote. Often this device or *hook* helps a writer introduce an idea. I have taken many quotes from a very useful book of quotations by Robert Fitzhenry (1993) and indicate this source with an asterisk (*).

Acknowledgments

I am indebted to my many doctoral students, who have taught me as much about writing dissertations as I have taught them.

Also, I was fortunate to receive varied and substantive criticism from others who have long worked with doctoral students. These are individuals who know research and doctoral education well. Their suggestions have made this book a far better resource for the doctoral student. Lastly, the contributions of the following reviewers are gratefully acknowledged:

Maria Piantanida, Ph.D.
Adjunct Associate Professor
University of Pittsburgh
Pittsburgh, PA

Mark H. Rossman, Ed.D.
Senior Faculty
Capella University
Minneapolis, MN

Allan Glatthorn
Author and Professor
(retired)
Washington, NC

Douglas Fisher
Associate Professor of
Teacher Education
San Diego State University
San Diego, CA

Susan Mintz
Coordinator of Secondary
Education
University of Virginia
Charlottesville, VA

Dr. Jody S. Britten
Assistant Professor
Department of Educational
Studies
Ball State University
Muncie, IN

Xiufeng Liu
Associate Professor of
Science Education
State University of New
York at Buffalo
Buffalo, NY

Tim Green, Ph.D.
Director of Distance
Education
Assistant Professor of
Elementary Education
California State University,
Fullerton
Fullerton, CA

Jon Margerum-Leys
Assistant Professor
Eastern Michigan University
Ypsilanti, MI

Leonard H. Elovitz
Coordinator of Graduate
Programs in Educational
Leadership
Kean University
Union, NJ

Susan Doran Quandt, Ed.D.
Director, Advising and
Academic Programs
Division of Graduate and
Continuing Education
Westfield State College
Westfield, MA

Sandra K. Enger, Ph.D.
Associate Professor of
Science Education
Associate Director, Institute
for Science Education
University of Alabama in
Huntsville
Huntsville, AL

About the Author

Miles T. Bryant is Professor in the Department of Educational Administration in Teachers College at the University of Nebraska—Lincoln. He earned his doctoral degree at Stanford University and became a member of the graduate faculty at the University of Nebraska—Lincoln. Like a number of doctoral-degree-granting institutions in the United States, the Teachers College at the University of Nebraska—Lincoln has made available to its doctoral students a special course in the construction of the dissertation proposal and dissertation. He has taught this course since 1992. Over this time period, he has worked with hundreds of doctoral students in education and the social sciences. He has also mentored many of his own students to the successful completion of the doctoral dissertation. He is active in the American Educational Research Association, has published numerous academic papers, and has edited several books. *The Portable Dissertation Advisor* is a book grounded in these years of experience.

1

First Steps Toward Your Dissertation

How to Use This Book

I try to take life one day at a time but sometimes several days attack me at once.

—Ashley Brilliant*

As they attempt to build a dissertation study, doctoral students in general and nontraditional students in particular often find themselves short of time and full of confusion. Doctoral students want very targeted information dealing with the particular issue or question about their study that they face. More often than not, these students want their information when they need it. Thus, it is appropriate to list a few shortcuts through this book.

If you would like to see the typical components of the doctoral dissertation proposal that are expected by faculty in many fields, turn to the Outline of a Proposal in Chapter 2, which outlines the standard convention of providing the first three chapters of your study. If you are at the point where you know your topic or general area and want to begin researching your topic, turn to Chapter 3, which provides

---

As mentioned in the Preface, I have taken many quotes from a book of quotations by Robert Fitzhenry (1993) and indicate this source with an asterisk (*).

much information about locating research literature. I have taken pains to try to give you insights into the special resource that the research library represents for your work. There is an index at the end of the book that should help you locate information about particular topics. Use the index as a guide to those topics in the book that you find of particular importance.

If you are at a point where you have not yet fixed on a topic, turn to the section in this chapter on Finding a Topic. It may help give you some ideas about how to identify a researchable topic for your study. Once you have settled on a topic, read the section titled Outline of a Proposal in Chapter 2. You may also wish to read Finding a Dissertation Support Group later in this chapter. There I discuss the benefits of creating a group of fellow students that become a support group for one another.

In the construction of the dissertation proposal or dissertation, realize that not all dissertations begin with the conventional first three chapters. Many qualitative, historical, or ethnographic studies, for example, stray from such conventions in their structure. Still, it is common for the proposal and the finished dissertation to contain an introductory chapter, a literature review chapter, and a methodology chapter.

It will be obvious as you use this book that I have made one important and essential assumption: The nontraditional student has to have the technology to communicate and to gather library resources. Indeed, some doctoral programs (the University of Florida at Gainesville, for example) require that doctoral students possess and use a computer. Coursework, advising, registration for courses, and access to programmatic information all are now commonly done via the Internet. E-mail is used to communicate with an advisor, committee members, and fellow students. If you do not have an up-to-date computer and access to both e-mail and the Internet, you will find many of the suggestions in this book of limited use. Indeed, if you lack these essential resources, it will be very difficult for you to complete your dissertation as a nontraditional student.

For example, accessing a research library is normally an essential part of constructing a dissertation. Students who cannot travel to such a library need Internet access to do this work. Nontraditional doctoral students usually must be very efficient with their use of time. Remote access to a research library will significantly increase your efficiency. If you form a dissertation support group, e-mail and chat rooms are significant assets. You need to be able to communicate with your advisor. E-mail facilitates this communication significantly. Computers are essential.

Browse through Appendix D at the conclusion of the book. In this index, I list many dissertations that have been written about the doctoral dissertation and doctoral experience. These are studies by fellow doctoral students of the very process in which you are engaged. You may well find studies you wish to read.

Dissertation Conventions

Don't ever take a fence down until you know why it was put up.

—Robert Frost*

Conventions

In this introductory section of the book, I provide an overview of the issues the doctoral student faces as she or he begins to construct a dissertation. My main purpose in Chapter 1 is to introduce the conventions that typically guide the construction and writing of the dissertation and to discuss the common issues the nontraditional student will experience at this stage of the process.

I use the word *conventions* to indicate commonly expected behaviors and dissertation components one will find in most doctoral programs most of the time. For the nontraditional student, an understanding of these conventions will save both time and energy in planning, researching, and writing. Much of the material of this book relates to conventions, from the utilization of a dissertation advisor to the required format of the finished document. And, as the quote from Robert Frost implies, it is important to know why these "fences" or conventions were "put up," especially if you intend to exclude one.

Conventions in This Section

Advisor
Supervisory Committee
Expectation of a Research Study
Solo Scholarship
Parts of the Dissertation Study
Literature Review
Method
Gathering of New Data or Information
Expectation of Objectivity

The doctoral dissertation is written for a very limited and unique audience—the student's doctoral advisor and the student's doctoral supervisory committee. This is one of the conventions that may be so obvious as to be taken for granted, but for the nontraditional student, a clear understanding of this convention is necessary. Any discussion of the conventions associated with writing a dissertation proposal must attend to the unique nature of the relationship between the student and the professors with whom that student must work. Attending to the personalities of the members of the supervisory committee is a responsibility of the doctoral student and the advisor. This is particularly challenging for the nontraditional doctoral student. Be alert to opportunities to learn about the professors on your committee. When you visit the campus, try to schedule time to meet with each. Look for Web sites that your committee members may have created. Interact with them by e-mail. Talk with fellow students.

Advisor

The doctoral student's advisor is a key factor in the whole doctoral program and becomes even more central when the student begins the dissertation. Convention reserves for this individual a great deal of practical authority over the dissertation of his or her advisees. The student learns that neither a dissertation proposal nor a dissertation will be advanced for approval without the full involvement and concurrence of the doctoral dissertation advisor.

Supervisory Committee

Another convention is the supervisory committee. This is a group of faculty members drawn from the student's major field and from other fields. This supervisory committee has been charged to uphold standards of scholarship and research imposed by the graduate faculty. In many institutions, this committee will consist of four professors with at least one of the members coming from another discipline, college, or school. The doctoral student will need the approval of this committee for any or all of the following: a preproposal, a dissertation proposal, passage of an oral examination on the dissertation, and, of course, the dissertation itself. You will note, as you read dissertations, a signature page that documents the approval of this committee.

Expectations Held for Degree

For the student, it is also important to come fully to grips with the expectations the academy holds for the doctoral degree. In most universities, the doctoral degree is highly regarded as a study that makes a contribution to learning. The degree signals the discovery of new knowledge. However, this goal is not always recognized in programs that have come to use the doctoral degree in part as a professional degree for career development. For example, many students that complete a degree in education or business do not contemplate academic careers. Doctoral study does afford intellectual growth and knowledge of the research in one's field. But a future academic career during which they will continue to discover new knowledge is not an expectation held by many nontraditional doctoral students. Accordingly, nontraditional students often value knowledge that has practical utility. Students in educational fields frequently want knowledge that will be of use in their professional area. Thus, there may be a dissonance between the traditional goal of the academy to produce the independent researcher and the goal of the 21st-century doctoral student to acquire practical knowledge that will aid in practice. For this reason, many of the conventions of the dissertation proposal phase can appear as unnecessary to the nontraditional doctoral student who has no intention of pursuing a career as a professor or researcher. However, it is a widely held expectation that the dissertation will add to the knowledge base of its field and train the student as a researcher.

Solo Scholarship

It is a conventional expectation that the recipient of the degree is to be understood as a person who has demonstrated a capacity to conduct independent research. Mortimer Adler speaks of a type of learning in which one accumulates knowledge by research, by investigation, and by reflection (Adler & van Doren, 1972). Such learning is independent of the direct or indirect assistance of another. This type of learning by discovery and reflection characterizes the work of the doctoral student engaged in constructing his or her dissertation proposal. While a doctoral student still learns under the tutelage of an advisor and the scrutiny of a doctoral committee, the knowledge gained in carrying out a dissertation is, in most cases, the result of discovery.

This distinguishing independence associated with the dissertation proposal and with the dissertation itself must be recognized quickly by the doctoral student. Most educational systems rely on "aided discovery" from a teacher in order to become expert in acquiring received knowledge (Adler & van Doren, 1972). Our education, even in graduate school, does not always train us to acquire knowledge through discovery. Such a trained incapacity to function as an independent scholar can often be a large obstacle in the way of the completion of the doctoral degree. Realize that you are now operating in a very different learning environment.

It is extremely important to make this psychological shift from thinking of yourself as a passive learner to thinking of yourself as an independent and active learner. The doctoral student writing the dissertation is almost always the initiator of action. There are no obligations to do an assignment or show up for class. There is no formal feedback along the way; the judgment comes when you turn in a proposal or a dissertation and it comes all at once. Dissertation learning is truly a different kind of learning. It is what I call solo scholarship.

There are instances where doctoral students work in teams or in pairs on common topics, but these experiences are uncommon.

The Literature Review

One of the most difficult of these conventions is the expectation or convention that professors refer to as the literature review. By this label, professors typically mean the scholarship that has been published by others about a particular topic of study. Logically, if a person is to invent new knowledge or generate new discoveries, he or she should know what has already been invented. But, an exhaustive review of the scholarship in a field does not always mesh with the goals of the doctoral student who may be more interested in using selected knowledge that appears to him or her to have widespread practical utility. The literature review is a very important dissertation convention.

Research Method

Another convention that appears in most graduate programs is an expectation that a well-designed methodology section be presented. Logically, if a person is to invent new knowledge, the process that will be followed in so doing should be indicated. Again, the doctoral student who is more interested in practical utility may find the requirement of a rigorous application of academic research standards to be less compelling than the creation of reportable results.

Gathering of New Data or Information

Finally, one of the key expectations behind the doctoral dissertation is that it will be a study that seeks to systematically gather information or data. In most institutions, professors expect that the doctoral study will contain a framework for gathering and analyzing new data. This is why doctoral students are often told to save their book about the way the world should work for another time. Few faculty members expect to read a dissertation study that is a polemic on the student's pet set of beliefs. There is an expectation that the study will seek to objectively analyze data or information that the student has gathered. There is an expectation that any conclusions or recommendations made by the student will spring only from the data or information presented in the dissertation. Thus, while many doctoral candidates may have knowledge of a topic or problem of practice that far exceeds their dissertation focus, that knowledge must not mask or supercede the data contained in the study.

Expectation of Objectivity

Most advisors and supervisory committee members expect the doctoral dissertation writer to strive for objectivity in approach and analysis. This does not mean that the writer must rigidly adhere to a positivistic standard that eschews any admission that personal beliefs may color the interpretation of what he or she discovers or sees in the data or information. The first-person voice, for example, has become much more widely used in recent years as qualitative dissertations have increased in number. However, even in qualitative dissertations, there is an expectation that the writer will be objective in proceeding with data analysis and conclusions. Few committees, as I point out later, will accept a personal polemic for a dissertation. Eisner, in his book *The Enlightened Eye*, has written an excellent discussion of issues of objectivity and subjectivity in research (1991, pp. 41–61).

Conventions such as these need to be understood.

It is important to emphasize another obvious convention. The proposal and dissertation are written scholarly documents. If one has a weakness in writing, this weakness will quickly show up. Errors in structure, grammar, and logical expression interfere with a reader's ability to track the meaning of the writer. Likewise, expert writing can help enormously in guiding the reader to an appreciation of the content of the proposal and dissertation. If you know you have a weakness as a writer, include in your planning some provision for serious help with editing your work. I should note that it is unethical to have another person write your study or even sections of your study. It is not unethical to have another person go over what you have written and make suggestions for improvement.

Summary

Realize then that the dissertation study is guided by the following conventions:

Conventions Summarized

1. There is an established supervisory structure.

2. The study is guided by research objectives and research questions.

3. The study is informed by what other scholars have discovered.

4. The study is designed to gather new data or to analyze preexisting data in new ways.

5. An objective analysis of gathered data is a goal.

6. Conclusions must arise from the data and information gathered.

7. The study will be judged by how thoroughly the research questions are answered.

8. Faculty expect the researcher will make recommendations for improved practice or future research.

9. Those recommendations must also arise from the data and information gathered.

Realize also that one may deviate from these conventions for cause. As I will discuss in the next section, clear communication with your advisor is necessary in all aspects of constructing the proposal and dissertation. The next section covers the mechanical process or chronology of constructing the dissertation. As might be anticipated, this process is also conventionalized. There are steps one goes through that are common to many doctoral-degree-granting institutions.

The Dissertation Process

I like terra firma—the more firma, the less terra.

—George Kaufman*

What steps does a person go through in constructing and completing the doctoral dissertation? As you might surmise, this process will vary from campus to campus, but there will also be general similarities. In this section, I lay out the usual pathway along which the doctoral student travels in conceptualizing, initiating, and completing the dissertation.

I begin with the most important resource the university provides you in the dissertation process—the doctoral advisor or supervisory committee chair.

Advisor–Advisee Relations

Most doctoral programs rely on a single faculty member to supervise the doctoral student's dissertation. Occasionally, a student will have cochairs or cosupervisors. This is sometimes done as a means of mentoring a faculty member new to doctoral advising. The advisor is typically the most important resource for the doctoral student. It is critical that you have open communication with this person, and it is critical that you feel you may speak openly with this person.

For a nontraditional student, establishing a working relationship with the advisor is not always easy. You will need to have that individual's active help when you need it. University graduate programs identify advisors at different stages in the doctoral student's program. At some institutions, the advisor is appointed at the beginning of the program. At others, the dissertation advisor is appointed or selected in the later stages of the student's program. In any event, when you, the doctoral student, begin the dissertation, you will have an advisor. Sustained phone or e-mail contact with this individual is extremely important.

Before the student can settle on the dissertation topic, the advisor needs to grant approval. Before the student can feel comfortable proceeding with a dissertation idea, the advisor and/or student must bring the topic and research plan to a faculty committee for approval. In this process of negotiating the various approvals the student will need along the way, the advisor is key. The advisor normally also serves as an advocate for the student, alerting the student to requirements, expectations, and potential problem areas.

But the nontraditional student may experience difficulties in establishing a working relationship with the advisor simply due to time and distance constraints.

Tip

It is worth the time, money, and effort to meet with your advisor as you plan your dissertation. Travel to the campus to do so. Make sure you have scheduled your visit so that you will be able to have sufficient time with this person. Plan to talk about your own work and your intellectual interests and possible research topics. Find out what your advisor plans to be doing during the time period when you will actively work on your dissertation. Will she or he be on leave? Will she or he be on duty during the academic terms when you will need assistance?

There are other simple things you can do to learn more about your advisor.

First, professors produce scholarly writing. This will be true of your advisor. You should know what your advisor has written. Your advisor also has a rich professional life that touches different associations, meetings, conventions, national groups, state groups, and professional colleagues. Educate yourself about this aspect of your advisor's work. Your advisor will have a curriculum vitae that will, in all likelihood, stretch for many pages. Secure a copy of this. If your advisor publishes a Web site, locate that site and learn what it contains. You may find ways to enrich your own work and study.

Second, unlike doctoral study in arts and sciences or engineering fields, many doctoral students in education and social sciences do not write their theses in the fields in which their advisors possess in-depth knowledge. This is becoming even more common as nontraditional students engage in solo scholarship. The model of the scholar working as a junior member of a research team and publishing his or her dissertation work from that joint activity does not hold for the typical nontraditional student. There are instances where nontraditional students do work as part of a group on a common topic, but this is the exception. Thus, your advisor will have a general knowledge of your topic but may not be thoroughly conversant with the work in that field. If you know this to be the case, you can help your advisor by identifying individuals that can serve as a resource for you. Discuss this issue with your advisor.

Third, you will want to have some idea about your advisor's work with other doctoral students. This type of information is harder to come by for the nontraditional student. Has the advisor been active in helping students complete their dissertations? Does the advisor have experience in working with other graduate faculty on supervisory committees? Is the advisor one who will work with you to fully evaluate your proposal prior to your submitting your dissertation work to the full supervisory committee? It is your advisor who is in the best position to help you assess the quality of your work.

In some institutions, a course, often called The Dissertation Proposal, is offered to help students work through the development of their proposal. If offered, such a course is an extremely useful opportunity for the doctoral student to engage in the iterative process that is typical of the creation of the dissertation proposal. The outline below delineates what most students experience as they begin the first stage of their dissertations—gaining approval to embark on a study.

Usual Conventional Steps in Creating a Dissertation Proposal

1. Formative Stage
   (Discussions with advisor, tentative writings)

2. Initial Determination of Topic
   (Repeated explorations and attempts to frame problem and research questions, serious reading on the proposed topic)

3. Initial Draft of Chapter One
   (Continued conversations with advisor, growing awareness of literature about topic)

4. Commitment to Topic
   (Implicit decision that the topic and focus is clear)

5. Writing Proposal Draft Including Literature Review
   (Submission to advisor, modifications)

6. Approval of Draft by Advisor
   (Communication with full committee)

7. Submission of Draft to Committee Members

8. Completion of Institutional Review Board (IRB) Application

9. Proposal Meeting

10. Modifications of Proposal

11. Committee Approval of Proposal

12. IRB Approval of Study

> **Tip**
>
> Who does what in terms of interacting with the supervisory committee as a whole? Do you take the lead? Does your advisor take the lead? Do you send the draft proposal to the committee? Does your advisor send the draft? Discuss these issues with your advisor.

The outline appears simple. Realize that each doctoral student experiences this process differently. For some, the determination of the topic is easy, the advisor has abundant time and energy to devote to the student, the rest of the faculty committee is helpful, the library works, and the whole proposal process falls in place smoothly. For others, the path is rocky.

The following sections capture some of the likely issues most doctoral students encounter as they seek to settle on a dissertation focus.

Finding a Topic

There's too much confusion here. I can't get no relief.

—"All Along the Watchtower," Bob Dylan*

What is my topic? Is it the right topic? Is it a doable topic? Do I have to like my topic? In this section, I discuss what for some is the single most difficult part of the dissertation process: selecting a topic and narrowing it down to a doable dissertation.

Choosing a dissertation topic is not always easy. In fact, sometimes the topic is as elusive as a will-o'-the-wisp. Yet people have written about so many different topics that, for the optimist, the ingenuity of the doctoral student will restore faith in human creativity. For the pessimist, the list of dissertation topics might confirm the absurdity of life. Here are a few remarkable titles (and order numbers) from the database of Dissertation Abstracts.

- Elvis Presley: All Shook Up (QVQ90-09636)
- Life's Little Problems . . . and Pleasures: Watching Soap Operas (QVQ91-02565)
- Electrical Measurements on Cuticles of the American Cockroach (QVQ66 08750)
- Determinants of Flossing Behavior in the College Age Population (QVQ83-21137)
- Classification of Drinking Styles Using the Topographical Components of Beer Drinking (QVQ82-07677)

- Garage Sales as Praxis: Ideologies of Women, Work, and Community in Daily Life (QVQ90-32549)
- Finger Painting and Personality Diagnosis (QVQ00-00801)
- Communication Use in the Motorcycle Gang (QVQ89-06234)
- Ritual Drama in American Culture: The Case of Professional Wrestling (QVQ89-18545)
- An Adaptive Surfing Apparatus (QVQ13-06897)
- I Am You, You Are Me: A Philosophical Explanation of the Possibility That We Are All the Same Person (QVQ86-28990)
- Jock and Jill: Aspects of Women's Sports History in America (QVQ79-10447)

Conventional Approach to Selecting a Topic

The classic approach to selecting a topic has been described as the deficiency approach. The doctoral student pores over the research literature, building a record of past research activity that eventually leads either to a topic that begs to be explored or to a topic that scholars identify as needing to be explored. It is common for doctoral students, at the conclusion of their dissertations, to recommend future research topics. Remember this convention as you search Dissertation Abstracts. You may well find your study in another doctoral student's dissertation. One scours the literature, including dissertations, for gaps in the knowledge base about a topic. This approach remains a valid way to identify a researchable dissertation topic.

Others come to their topic based on professional or personal experience. And still others have advisors or research opportunities that place a topic in their path. Each student's dissertation journey is unique.

> **Tip**
>
> Talk with others about your dissertation idea and not just other students. Talk to those who have nothing to do with the university. Talk to your family members and relatives, your fellow employees, your mechanic, your mail person. The more widely you converse about your topic, the clearer you will be about it.

Narrowing the Focus and Finding Clarity

To some, everybody else's study seems so perfect and clear while their own study idea seems murky and unfocused. While it is perhaps of little comfort, the lack of focus is common. The dissertation topic almost always has to be narrowed to a point where the student has identified a suitable dissertation study. This is best done in an iterative manner in which one tries out ideas for topics. Presenting these ideas to others allows for refinement and focus.

Example of Narrowing the Focus

A student wants to study emotional intelligence as an important skill in nurses. She intends to do a survey of nurses. Through ongoing discussions, she realizes that in some areas of nursing, emotional intelligence may simply not be of particular importance, while in other areas, there is a logical and compelling need to be gifted in this particular type of human intelligence. She narrows her focus to concentrate on pediatric nurses.

At times, this iterative process is done with the advisor. For the nontraditional student, access to an advisor may be done via e-mail exchanges and with phone conversations. But in programs with large numbers of doctoral students, the advisor may simply be unable to afford concentrated time with an advisee, and the nontraditional student may find it difficult to sustain a series of conversations with the advisor about the topic. Consequently, proposal classes or peer support groups can be of real benefit to helping the student both select and refine a topic.

There are both mental and procedural steps that a doctoral student can take in traversing this stage of selecting a topic. Below I cover issues that frequently surface during the stage in which the student seeks to commit to the topic of the study.

Prepare for Uncertainty and Change

First, most doctoral candidates go down a crooked path on the way to their dissertation topic. There are frequent forks in the road. Frost's poetic reminiscence of how he took the road less traveled and "that has made all the difference" does not necessarily hold for the selection of doctoral dissertation topics. Sometimes a student is following a deep trail worn by early scholars all exploring an important topic. Sometimes, following the deep path made by earlier generations of scholars is a good idea. The replication of earlier studies is important. A rich body of knowledge about a topic can often lead to clarity.

Second, it is common to change the focus of the dissertation study a number of times. You might write the research purpose and questions one day only to modify them the next day. It often takes much writing to discover meaning before the study takes shape. You can generally believe that the final focus has been identified when a firm commitment has been made. An apt analogy is that of a marriage. When you feel a commitment to a course of action, you become firmly attached or engaged to it. You feel no sense of uncertainty or discomfort with what you propose to do. You no longer feel it necessary to search for additional refinements. Furthermore, when others suggest you do a different study but you are able to successfully adhere to your topic, you are on solid ground. As this commitment solidifies, it will mean not only that you have selected a focus and topic but also that you have found a topic that will sustain your interest.

Some students, passionately wishing to complete their doctoral programs, will select what is referred to as a *doable* topic. This is perhaps more common than faculty advisors would care to admit. There is nothing wrong with expedience as the basis for arriving at a topic. Realize, however, that even though the topic may have been selected for completely pragmatic reasons, you must sustain your interest in the topic for a period of time. Murphy's Law (if it can go wrong, it will) almost inevitably surfaces during the dissertation process, so your interest in seeing the research project through to conclusion must survive both time and adversity.

Beware of Gift Topics

Sometimes your advisor, your employer, or convenience presents a possible topic to you. If you are working with your advisor on a research project, the selection process will take care of itself. In most instances, your advisor and his or her research agenda will carry you through to completion. When it is an employer that influences or seeks to dictate the selection of a dissertation topic, issues arise. Because the great majority of nontraditional doctoral students in the social sciences and in education work while they study, it is common for doctoral students to try to identify a dissertation that will have some utility in their work setting. In some instances, such an arrangement works and the student reaps multiple benefits. Often, however, the needs of the work setting and the nature of doctoral study are incompatible.

Assume you are a full-time curriculum coordinator in a large school district that has been wrestling with declining reading scores in its elementary schools. You have been directed to develop a plan for improving these reading scores. You want the plan you develop to serve as your dissertation. You propose this to your advisor. Your advisor asks, "What is your research problem? What is your research question?" You respond that your district wants a curriculum plan. Your advisor responds that a "plan" is not a problem. The creation of a curriculum plan is not guided by a set of researchable questions unless you explore the underlying issues.

The problem implicit in your proposed study is declining reading scores.

Thus, your advisor might suggest that you design a pre–post study to measure the impact of the proposed curriculum to improve reading. You would then need to gather performance data from students and subject this data to analysis to see if the new curriculum had any impact in arresting the decline in reading achievement.

The doctoral student who proposes to examine his or her own work or own program presents a similar type of problem. Creswell (1998) referred to this as conducting research in "one's own backyard" and cautioned against such a practice. An example might be the student who conducts specific professional development workshops for nonprofit organizations and wants to gather data from the participants about the efficacy of these workshops and their content. Perhaps a teacher has developed a particular approach to teaching and wants to study its effect in increasing student achievement scores, or perhaps a distance education doctoral student wants to study why fellow students in his program persist or drop out.

There are some obvious issues in terms of the relationship of both the researcher to the subjects and the researcher to the object of the study. The researcher can be expected to have a particular interest in interpreting data in ways that support the judgments he or she has already made about his or her backyard. In metaphoric terms, the danger is that the researcher may be salting the research mine. That is, like the crooked real estate agent trying to pass a piece of property off as being of greater value than it is, the researcher runs the risk of selectively valuing some data because these data serve his or her biases. The message is to beware of topics that arise from work. As James Thurber (1956) wrote, "You can't make anything out of cookie dough but cookies." You may only get work out of the effort to combine the dissertation with a work-related project. Please note that some qualitative researchers will disagree with me on this point—Behar (1996) for example.

In a similar fashion, we are frequently tempted to take advantage of preexisting data. Fortune brings our way a whole set of completed data on subjects. What we lack is a question or questions to ask of these data. So, in an effort to jump-start a dissertation topic, we decide to fashion a question for which we know there are answers in the data set. This works sometimes. Numerous studies, for example, have been conducted using the large national, longitudinal data sets like the High School and Beyond data (http://nces.ed.gov/surveys/hsb/).

Data sets of this nature were designed with educational research in mind. However, as often as we are able to find institutional data sets that we see as a convenient source of a dissertation topic, just as often, those data are mainly descriptive and provide little basis for a theoretical study. If you begin with an issue, problem, or theoretical concern and then search for existing data sets that might be a reasonable source for information, you will have a more coherent study. Some dissertation committees operate by an unwritten rule that requires the doctoral study to develop the context and the research questions prior to the identification of how relevant data and information will be gathered. If you are considering the use of preexisting data that you do not have to compile, make sure you have spoken to your advisor about this intention.

> ## Tip
>
> It is easy to get demographic data about research subjects. All too often, demographic data constitute the only independent variables a researcher uses to predict variation in dependent variables. As a consequence, race, gender, age, and socioeconomic status are presented as the most important factors influencing the dependent variable. Just because these variables are easy to get does not mean they are necessarily of much value. If you intend to use such variables, make sure that you have plumbed the research literature for the theoretical basis that identifies the importance of race, gender, age, and socioeconomic status to your particular topic.

Don't Try to Save the World

"My study will teach teachers how to create in the student internal and intrinsic motivation to learn." So wrote a graduate student some years ago as he began to put a proposal together. Eventually this study became an investigation of the "effects of students' attitudes toward school when competition for grades was removed from their classroom experience" (Guenzel, 1993). The first purpose was grand and worthy. It was too large an exploration for a dissertation. The second was much more focused in scope. In constructing your proposal, set your target on a research setting or population that you can explore.

Your work has a chance to be perceived as highly significant when you set out to explore a timely and debated area in your discipline or field of study. If your dissertation topic is likely to be of great interest to other scholars and likely to be well received in competitive research journals and conferences, you increase the chances that what you discover will have an impact. Some students use their dissertation as the foundation for future professional activities, taking the knowledge from the study and using it to develop programs to help practitioners improve practice.

Don't Pick a Topic That Will Solve a Personal Issue

There is little point in going through all of the complexity and effort of designing a doctoral dissertation if you already know the answer to your research question. Usually when we have adopted a strong position on an issue or a problem of practice, we are operating from a set of beliefs. It is hard to shake our beliefs loose from their moorings. And, whatever data we gather are likely to be put together in such a way that they reinforce our beliefs. This is hardly the best starting point for a study that is supposed to be an objective piece of scholarship that is based on data and adds new knowledge to the field.

For example, the delivery of university coursework via distance education has received much attention lately. One doctoral student, convinced by argument and personal experience, wanted to demonstrate that distance learning was a much better way to learn than regular face-to-face instruction. Buttressed with arguments untested by empirical study, this dissertation set out to prove the superiority of distance learning by interviewing students who had taken distance-learning coursework for their doctoral degree. Eventually, the study came to focus on the experiences of faculty members who designed distance courses in faculty teams, and the issue of proving the superiority of distance learning was abandoned.

Another study that posed problems for its author sought to study the efficacy of an approach to the teaching of reading. This researcher was quite vested in a phonics-based approach that he had designed and sought to examine its success in a classroom. The classroom was the researcher's classroom. The teacher designed and implemented the intervention. In such a design, it is difficult to save the researcher from the researcher. The study could have shifted to a qualitative examination of the lived experiences of the teacher in trying to implement a change. Such a shift would turn the obvious personal bias into a strength by shifting the focus to a qualitative study of the teacher's own experiences. It is difficult to study oneself but some dissertations have, in fact, done so to good effect (e.g., Heaton, 1994).

Try to avoid a topic in which you have a clear and vested interest. James Thurber provides the following wry thought: "Get it right or let it alone. The conclusions you jump to may be your own" (1956). One should let the data and evidence have some say in the results of the study.

> **Tip**
>
> In doing any sort of study that relies upon you as the source of data and information, your committee will want you to discuss the issue of bias. How will you guard against allowing your personal views to distort your data? How might your personal experience and values be an asset if you intend your study to contain personal narrative and experiences? Remember, the dissertation convention expects objectivity. If your study purpose and design set this convention aside, be prepared to defend your choice.

Pick a Topic That Will Be of Service to Your Field

If, after you complete your study, you present your research to a professional or scholarly assembly, will anybody come to your presentation? If the answer is yes (as best you can guess), then you have selected a topic that has relevance to your professional colleagues. In this regard, you must read voraciously. Look up dissertations in Dissertation Abstracts. Search on the online electronic databases like ERIC. Look at what has been presented at scholarly research meetings such as the American Educational Research Association's annual meeting.

Your dissertation is unlikely to be of much service to your

> **Tip**
>
> Identify those national research associations that encompass your academic area and your dissertation topic. Search the program of their annual meetings for topics in your area. If you find closely related presentations by other scholars, consider calling them and talking with them about your work. Researchers, even the most distinguished of scholars, are normally quite open to such conversations with those who share their interests.

> ### Tip
>
> The annals of doctoral research are full of examples of doctoral students and advisors presenting research and publishing papers together. Discuss this possibility with your advisor early in your dissertation efforts. You will profit from such a discussion by learning more about publishing research. In addition, publications are the highly valued currency in the realm of the university, so your advisor may well be especially interested in such opportunities.

field if it sits unread on your shelf. It used to be the case that a doctoral student expected to publish papers from his or her dissertation. This is still an expectation in a number of fields. For the nontraditional student who does not plan a career as a research scholar, the pressure to publish from the dissertation is decreased. Still, if your study is of worth, it deserves a wider audience than your advisor and supervisory committee. Thus, as you begin your study, consider what sort of a product you might produce from it. Perhaps you will want to publish several scholarly papers for research journals or practitioner journals. Perhaps you will want to create a book from your study. The practice of professionals in the education and social science fields is increasingly built upon a foundation of research. In the field of education, this is sometimes referred to as *best practice.* The most recent federally funded school reform effort (No Child Left Behind) requires that funded projects be grounded in research as a condition of funding. This promises to enhance the utilization of research activities such as dissertation studies in education. In professional fields, there has always been a need for research that has clear implication for practice. Thus, consider what value your work may have in helping professionals improve their work, and consider how you will get your news to these professionals.

Summary

Prepare to read voraciously as a means of settling on your dissertation topic. Talk about your intentions with lots of people. Write to discover. Read other doctoral dissertations. Attend national conferences that have sessions relating to your interests. If your institution has a course designed to help you construct the dissertation proposal or dissertation, sign up for that course. Be patient. The topic will come to you.

Finding a Theory

Data data everywhere but not a thought to think.

—Theodore Rosak*

This section offers a lengthy discussion of one of the difficult topics the nontraditional student faces—the place of theory in the doctoral dissertation. I devote space to this topic because I have found the use of theory to be perplexing to many nontraditional students.

The ubiquitous symbol that Nike developed, the Swoosh, serves as an icon for our age. "Just do it!" This icon says to us at one level that we should not worry about why we do something. It is more important to act than it is to reason about why we act. If we think too long about our behavior, we run the risk of not risking, of not acting. The slogan is both a call for mindlessness and an expression of cultural impatience.

Doctoral students are sometimes infected by the urge to just do it (get the dissertation done) and by the feelings of impatience that often accompany the slow process of designing and completing the dissertation. Still, masterful as the Nike slogan is as a marketing tool for a company that wants to sell shoes, it does not serve as a useful mantra for the doctoral dissertation writer. All dissertations, like all practice, are predicated on beliefs. Put another way, all dissertations explicitly or implicitly arise from theories about the way things work. The degree to which a dissertation author uses or recognizes theory will vary widely.

For nontraditional doctoral students who have not spent a great deal of time being socialized into academic life at the university, there can be many aspects to doctoral study that appear strange and mysterious. One of those pieces of doctoral research that may seem abstract and difficult to grasp is the notion that the dissertation is expected to spring from some theoretical perspective. What is a theory? Do I have to build my study using some kind of theory? What if I just want to gather some data and see what these data tell me? How do I use a theory in framing my research questions? Does the theory come first or do the questions come first?

If a person reads through the dissertation abstracts in the research library, one will soon note that many of these research studies fall into the category of descriptive studies. Sometimes students use the useful term *exploratory* as a means of signaling that their study does not test a theoretical hypothesis. The key elements of such studies are that the researchers gather data of either a quantitative or a qualitative type, present those data, and discuss the data in limited ways. The analysis and interpretation of these data usually is limited to the perceptions the researcher can bring to the task. There may be a noticeable lack of comment and insight from other scholars. There will be little utilization of a theoretical perspective as the foundation of the study.

What do female educational leaders say about their experiences attaining leadership positions? What are the factors school superintendents describe as important in their relationships with school boards? What factors influence classroom teachers to resist inclusion as a classroom practice? What factors influence at-risk college students to remain in college? What institutional behaviors do minority college students perceive as barriers to completion? Does a particular set of clinical practices change the communication patterns of autistic children? If these researchers used some set of beliefs to attempt to answer these questions, their studies would be grounded in theory. If they sought to build a theory about behavior from data they gathered, their studies would be labeled as grounded theory studies. If they simply sought to describe perceptions or factors with no effort to advance or test an idea or an explanation, these studies would be atheoretical. That is, the researchers neither set out to explore a theory nor utilized any particular theoretical perspective in arriving at their conclusions.

> Much philosophical controversy has centered on how to draw the distinction between the observable and the unobservable. Did Galileo observe the moons of Jupiter with his telescope? Do we observe bacteria under a microscope? Do physicists observe electrons in bubble chambers? Do astronomers observe the supernova explosions with neutrino counters? Do we observe ordinary material objects or are sense-data the only observables?
>
> —Robert Audi, *The Cambridge Dictionary of Philosophy*

Audi's quote suggests to us that there is much about the world we cannot know with certainty. Thus, we develop explanations. Einstein suggested that we should imagine a clock encased in a box. We cannot open the box to see the clock in action, but we can observe its actions. Understanding the elements that lead to that action involves theory. Many dissertation studies begin with a theory that is intended to explain action prior to the gathering of data or utilize theory in seeking to explain what has been observed.

I begin my own work with doctoral students with a theory. My theory is this. Practice is based on theory (or belief) whether we choose to recognize this or not. If this idea of mine is true, then all of our explorations into practice are based on our beliefs, on our theories about why we and others do what we do. When a school administrator instructs a teacher to gain more control and discipline in her classroom, that instruction is based on a set of beliefs about schooling and learning. When a teacher utilizes study centers in a fifth-grade classroom, the teacher does so because of implicit or explicit beliefs about what makes for effective learning. When a student of higher education studies different financial programs to learn what appears to best attract new students, that study is predicated on a set of beliefs about external incentives. When a social worker insists that family involvement in decision making is essential to long-term results, that conviction arises from a set of beliefs. When a special education professional uses animals as a motivator for autistic children, she or he does so because of implicit beliefs in what works for certain types of children. Indeed, our very choices about what to study in the doctoral dissertation are influenced by our beliefs about what matters. It is sometimes hard work to find the theories that do guide our work, but if we do not begin with some attempt to plumb our beliefs or the beliefs of others, we run the risk of contributing little to the understanding of others.

An illustration about the influence of theory follows. In 1968, Robert Rosenthal and Lenore Jacobson published the results of a study they had completed of teacher expectations. The two believed that when teachers expected high achievement from a student, that student's performance would rise to the expectation of the teacher. Conversely, if the teacher held limited expectations for the student, that student's performance would reflect that low expectation. Rosenthal and Jacobson were operating on a theory called expectancy theory. This theory guided their exploration into teacher behavior. Their study, *Pygmalion in the Classroom: Teacher Expectations and Pupils' Intellectual Development*, added to our knowledge of how formalized learning in schools can be better organized to promote student achievement (Rosenthal & Jacobson, 1968).

While Rosenthal and Jacobson did not invent the theoretical concept that guided their exploration, they did apply it to an educational setting. Expectancy theory was a notion that resonated with teachers and educational researchers. In the decades since this study was conducted, expectancy theory has spawned generations of curriculum developers and instructional specialists who stream out like missionaries to the school districts of the nation, armed with the idea or theory that if you think a child will do better, she or he will do better.

I offer this research as an example of how a belief in the way that the world works guided the exploration of a research project. This is what a theory does.

Here is another example of a theory. Alfie Kohn's work provides us with another equally useful but challenging set of assumptions about what works in classrooms and schools. Kohn (1999) challenged the prevailing belief that rewards serve to motivate the learner to learn. "Many of us," Kohn wrote, "believe motivation is direct: I tell you to do this and you will be rewarded. If the reward is sufficient, you will do what I ask." "Do this, and you will get that!" is Kohn's succinct summary of this belief that one will perform based on an expectation of some external reward like grades. Kohn offers us a competing theory. Internal rewards are more powerful motivators for learning. Rewards have a negative value in encouraging long-term motivation to learn and be creative. Acting in expectation of external rewards quickly becomes a matter of acting for the reward. In such instances, intrinsic motivation suffers. Kohn offers us a theory that we can systematically test by observing what works and what does not work.

Theory is a word derived from the Greek *theoria*, meaning "act of viewing, contemplating, considering." One of the early meanings of the word was that of the imaginative contemplation of reality. For Plato, a theory was a contemplated truth, a universal aspect of some thing. For Aristotle, a theory was pure knowledge, an abstraction of practice.

Theory causes confusion in the landscape of dissertation construction. Here are my suggestions for how to integrate theory into the doctoral dissertation. First, since your study may have its inspiration from the experiences you have had, begin by taking an inventory of the explanations that have been developed to account for the behavior or phenomenon in which you are interested. Such an approach requires that you dig beyond your own beliefs. Reading the literature about the subject that interests you will help you identify various explanations.

Second, think about how you might use these theories to guide the process you use to search for information and that you will use to help you interpret information once you have gathered it. The subject you intend to explore has probably been explained by competing theories, especially if the subject has been the object of study by generations of scholars. Think about causes. If you look at the outcomes or results of human or organizational behavior that interest you, try to identify some of the causes that lead to those outcomes.

Summary

Theory can provide you with a real focus that will go a long way toward helping you build a solid and coherent dissertation study. This does not mean you have to ground your study in theory or that you have to interpret your data according to some theory. The use of theory will, however, increase the probability that your study will make a contribution to your field and profession.

Finding a Research Method

I want a house that has gotten over all its troubles. I don't want to spend the rest of my life bringing up a young and inexperienced house.

—Jerome K. Jerome*

Like Jerome's inexperienced house, you may not want a research method (the process for answering your research questions) that has yet to get over all its troubles. In other words, you want a process that is clear, that gives you guidance for the collecting and analyzing of data, and that promises to provide you with a certain level of confidence that the conclusions you reach are based on a reasonably objective process.

Constructing the right process and procedure to address your research question is a matter of great consequence for your study. Many students find themselves attracted to a method before they know exactly what they wish to study. Students averse to statistics announce that they will do a qualitative study. Students comfortable with mathematics determine early that they have no patience for the fieldwork of the ethnographer. In both instances, the cart is going before the horse. The method you elect should be more determined by the purpose of the study and the question(s) that are to be answered and less determined by your taste for or aversion to a particular method.

If you have begun your study with a problem, then your research question(s) will be framed around that problem. If it is a problem that affects a particular population in some particular way, you can develop either a qualitative or a quantitative approach in order to answer your questions. If you elect the former, you may be able to make some valid recommendations relative to this population. If you elect a qualitative approach, you may be able to provide this population with some interesting perceptions. Using quantitative methodology, you may be able to speak with some authority about your target population. Using qualitative methodology, you may speak with authority about the experiences of those in your study. This extrapolation of the experiences of your subjects may provide meaningful information to others.

However, the method you select should also be influenced by the nature of the question(s) you ask.

While I have painted the preferred way to go, I know that it will remain the case that students will often select their method based on factors other than their research question(s). Their comfort levels with either quantitative or qualitative methods, the amount of time they have to devote to gathering data, the expenses associated with gathering data, and the skill level of the student in carrying out a method—all will be factors in the decision about finding a research method.

Summary

Be thoughtful and intentional about your choice of a research method. Make sure you have your research questions well formed before you settle on the method. Seek help from others about the options you have for addressing your research question(s). Consider at least two or three different design approaches. Read about research methods. Check out the research texts in the annotated bibliography in Appendix A.

Finding a Dissertation Support Group

Asking a working writer what he thinks about critics is like asking a lamppost how it feels about dogs.

—Christopher Hampton*

Good, constructive criticism is fundamental in building a sound dissertation. Such criticism may be unpleasant, as the quote above implies, but it is important. How does the nontraditional student create opportunities for such criticism?

For the nontraditional student, an informal peer group can be just the right antidote to the liability of what I have labeled solo scholarship. Solo scholarship is just what the label implies; it is researching and analyzing in isolation. Solo scholarship is a reality for most doctoral students at the dissertation stage, but that reality doesn't always lead to the best of outcomes. A lively focus on a research project by a number of people will typically result in a richer study. For example, a recent book titled *The Sociology of Philosophies*, by Randall Collins, finds that most major creations and innovations were brought to fruition within some kind of a movement or social group (Collins, 1998). If creativity was nourished socially for Freud, Degas, Hegel, Darwin, and Saturday Night Live, as Collins argues, creativity can be nurtured in the doctoral student by social interactions (Gladwell, 2002). Criticism of the right kind is essential in the construction and completion of a dissertation.

One of the best places to get criticism of the right kind is from a supportive group of peers. Students who pursue their degrees on campus or close enough to attend face-to-face classes often find ways to work together. When these students are all at the point of developing a doctoral dissertation, an opportunity exists for what graduate faculty now refer to as a dissertation support group, an informal group analogous to the class or course in the development of the dissertation proposal. Such interactive peer groups can go a long way toward replicating the type of experience many on-campus students find as they work to complete the dissertation.

Benefits of a Dissertation Support Group

The benefits of a peer support group are many. Psychologically it can be an important boost to be able to share issues, concerns, and doubts with others who are in a similar position. Shared experiences help the doctoral student overcome the obstacles that stand in the way. Dissertation support groups also tend to create a form of overt and covert pressure to work on the dissertation. This pressure is overt in that members of the group will typically help you improve your ideas and encourage you to move ahead. The pressure is covert in that you will feel a pressure to have something to communicate to the other members of the group about your progress.

A dissertation support group also gives you the weight of a larger group of students in dealing with the doctoral faculty and program administration. Often, nontraditional students suffer from not being able to voice their concerns or questions with professors. This is not due to intent. Faculty and program administrators have multiple demands on their time and the most immediate demand often receives the most attention. Thus, the nontraditional student may not feel well served by the institution.

A dissertation support group also provides students with the opportunity to practice developing clarity and rigor in their study. Having to present and defend your ideas before an audience is a solid way to bring strength to a dissertation study.

Organizing a Support Group

As you go through your program, you become familiar with other students. Either in face-to-face classes or in distance classes, you will have had an opportunity to come in contact with others. Your program may facilitate the formation of such support groups. If so, take advantage of this. If not, find ways to form your own. Ask your advisor about peer group support. You will be able to identify your fellow students by requesting names from the program administration or from class lists. Often, distance classes provide you with the names and e-mail addresses of others. Communicate with these individuals about forming a dissertation support group.

> **Tip**
>
> If at all possible, arrange for face-to-face meetings. All will benefit.

Who, how, and when are three factors you will want to keep in mind.

What students will be in your group? For on-campus groups, there is often the opportunity to know students from other doctoral programs, and thus the support group may consist of individuals from different programs. The nontraditional student tends to know best those students from the same department or program. It is probably best to begin with students in your program, although there may well be reason to involve others. It is also best to keep in mind that the group should consist of three to five students. The question of how to form a support group may require assistance from a faculty member or a program administrator. Establishing communication links is necessary. When to form a support group depends on need. Doctoral students at the dissertation stage can most benefit from such a group. Prior to that stage, there may be limited interest in devoting scarce time to an activity that does not seem relevant. Still, if you have worked in a class with others on a project, you might well have developed relationships that you value that could easily lead to a dissertation support group. Here are some suggested steps in forming a dissertation support group:

1. Identify students with whom you would like to work.

2. Either extend a specific invitation to students whom you know and respect to form a group of three to five students, or extend a more general invitation to the larger list of your peers, inviting all who wish to express their interest in participating in such a group.

3. Consider proximity in constructing a group (i.e., if possible, do you want people who can meet face to face?).

4. Consider personality (as best you can) in constructing such a group.

5. Consider how you will communicate and interact.

6. Give initial consideration to how often you will commit to interacting.

Getting Started

Here are some suggestions for beginning the work of the group. Below is a list of items to discuss. You can do so via e-mail, a chat room, a phone conference, or if possible, a face-to-face meeting.

1. Provide each member a chance to talk about his or her dissertation study.

2. Discuss what you want to accomplish as a group.

3. Discuss how you want to organize your group.

4. Discuss what you need to do to establish both asynchronous and synchronous ways to communicate (in all probability, you will want both).

5. Determine how you feel about establish for each other.

6. Determine how you feel about other people joining your group.

7. Determine how you want to achieve a supportive but critical environment.

I present specific activities for the support group in Appendix D.

Summary

Persistence is one of the characteristics that distinguishes those who complete their doctoral degrees from those who remain ABD (all but dissertation). Finding ways to persist is important. Obviously, how students organize their time and energy is important. A dissertation support group of peers can be an invaluable tool in helping you persist to completion.

The Doctoral Dissertation in Historical Perspective

Universities are the cathedrals of the modern age. They shouldn't have to justify their existence by utilitarian criteria.

—David Lodge*

This section provides the nontraditional student with general information about the basic convention of the dissertation itself. As doctoral education becomes more a part of professional preparation, there is a need to understand the origins of the doctoral dissertation in the scholarly academy. This section is written for those interested in the dissertation as a scholarly convention.

In any given year, it is common for U.S. institutions of higher education to award over 45,000 doctoral degrees in various fields and subject area disciplines. This is a large number that grows each year. Sheer numbers tax the institutions and faculty that provide the education that leads to these degrees. Table 1.1 presents information about doctoral degrees just in education.

For the student and the faculty advisor, the most challenging part of the degree program is the dissertation. Berelson noted that the doctoral dissertation stands at the center of the many issues associated with doctoral study (1960, p. 172). Matters have not changed in the years since that comment was made. Completing the dissertation is the stumbling block for many. It is often the first significant research project a student has attempted. It is often the first time in a person's educational career that learning is undertaken as such a solo activity. Completing the dissertation is often attempted against a backdrop of personal and employment obligations that constantly disrupt the study.

There have been significant changes in doctoral study over recent years. Both the nature of the experience and the students who

Table 1.1 Number of Doctoral Degrees in Education by Decade Using Subject Identifiers

	1960-1971	1971-1980	1981-1990	1991-2000
Educational Administration	636	1,880	5,572	6,168
Curriculum & Instruction	138	5,723	7,620	12,526
Education	32,228	73,079	75,228	86,333

Data Source: Dissertation Abstracts.

undertake the completion of a dissertation have changed in many ways. In order to understand the magnitude of these changes, it is helpful to recall the origins of doctoral study and doctoral dissertations.

Those who study higher education find that a university revolution occurred in the last part of the 19th century. During this time period, professors at places like Johns Hopkins, the University of Chicago, Harvard, Columbia, and Yale created the model of graduate programs that we know today. In the 19th century, many university officials advocated for graduate study, but resistance to innovation and disagreement over what graduate education should be provided much discussion. Several factors pushed the creation of new graduate programs and colleges. New fields of knowledge were creating great pressure on the classical curriculum. Significant numbers of U.S. students, dissatisfied with the classical offerings of U.S. universities, were studying abroad. Advanced study also had inherent appeal to many. Berelson (1960) provided an apt characterization of the shift in post-secondary education during this time period.

Prior to 1876, the following characteristics described U.S. post-secondary education:

1. The college positioned at the top of the educational hierarchy

2. A largely ministerial faculty (often a faculty drummed out of their church congregations)

3. A recitative class session as the pedagogical model

4. A small student body selected for gentility and social status

5. An unearned master's degree given to alumni for good behavior

6. Advanced students who went abroad

After 1900, the following characteristics prevailed:

1. The university at the top of higher educational hierarchy

2. Utilitarian and community-centered programs of study

3. New subjects of study

4. Seminars, labs, and dissertations added to pedagogical array

5. A growing attractiveness for new class of students

6. A graduate faculty

One hundred years later, doctoral education is again experiencing significant change. One can make the following list of new challenges to the type of doctoral education that was developed in 1900:

1. New providers, including corporations and proprietary organizations, are challenging the university monopoly over doctoral education.

2. Increasing numbers of part-time students stress the traditional graduate system.

3. Program administrators increasingly attempt to allow non-graduate faculty a role in assisting doctoral students.

4. The doctoral degree in some fields, particularly in education, is becoming less grounded in theory and more rooted in practice.

5. Students are demanding a greater customer orientation by doctoral programs in terms of access and expectations for practices in keeping with adult learners.

6. Faculty members witness a decline in the socialization of the student into the academy and discipline.

The traditional model of graduate education in which a graduate student works closely with a graduate faculty member is less common in many disciplines. Bronfenbrenner and Juravich (2000) wrote, "Gone is the hallowed tradition of graduate students as apprentice scholars, privileged to work closely with the greatest minds of their universities—and armed with the promise that upon completion of their apprenticeship they will gain a seat alongside their mentors in that lofty ivory tower" (p. 24). These changes have naturally altered the dissertation process experienced by the student.

The students who receive these degrees have changed as well. When the academy first invented doctoral dissertations, the common practice was that these students came to the university and studied there. More often than not, these doctoral students of earlier generations studied for many years. They labored in libraries and laboratories; they read deeply in their fields. Their doctoral studies were incubated slowly. Once they commenced their study, the collection of data and its analysis was labor intensive over an extended period of time. This depiction of the experience of earlier generations of doctoral students is probably not entirely accurate. If a person were to look at past dissertations, he or she would find many that show little evidence of this imagined type of rigor. Still, the image of the doctoral student cloistered in study for many years remains as an ideal.

The word *dissertation* comes from the Latin word *disserere*, meaning to discuss, treat, or examine. The *Oxford English Dictionary* identifies an early use of the word in an essay by Hobbes from 1651: "A dissertation concerning man in his severall habitudes and respects."

Other early writers also used the term:

Observing this, I made pause in my dissertation. (Dryden, 1783)

He composed three dissertations in a week, all on different subjects. (Pope, 1728)

Warton has expressly written a dissertation on the subject. (D'Israeli, 1841)

The sermone is a dissertation and does violence to nature in the effort to be like a speech. (Gladstone, 1879)

In these, as in most other contexts, the word dissertation means a spoken or written discussion of a particular topic. As professors at those U.S. institutions who set forth the new shape of graduate education debated what requirements they would impose upon students, one component that was quickly resolved was that of the dissertation. Students earning a doctoral degree would write and defend a dissertation. This was done in the expectation that such a requirement would help serve the goal of producing new knowledge and original thinkers. Thus the dissertation was established as the culminating experience of the doctoral student.

Today, as doctoral study becomes increasingly connected to professional development in many social science and business fields, some question why the writing of a dissertation is necessary. What sense is there in requiring a student to write a large academic research paper? Responses from the academy in defense of the dissertation vary, but here are some of the arguments. First, the doctoral degree is a research degree even in a professional program in education or business. Such degrees are granted by a governing board upon the recommendation of a graduate college or by the faculty of a college. As such, that academic community shapes degree requirements. The graduate faculty of a university controls what students must do in order to earn a degree. The dissertation is expected to demonstrate mastery of the field and to advance or to modify former knowledge; that is, it should analyze new material, find new results, or draw new conclusions. It may interpret old material in a new light.

Summary

This section has covered some of the underlying expectations of university faculty for the dissertation. Because the nontraditional student does not always have the luxury of assimilating this type of knowledge through a sustained campus presence, the underlying assumptions faculty hold for the dissertation study were covered. You should now have a better understanding of why you have been asked to design and carry out a dissertation study. The next five chapters of the book delineate the actual component parts of a dissertation and describe each.

2

The Introductory Sections

The Outline of a Proposal

Hear this: You cannot begin writing early enough.

—Harry Wolcott, 1995

There is an outline common to most dissertation proposals that the graduate faculty in many universities employ. This chapter will cover the features of that outline. There are obvious reasons for these structural conventions. The reader wants to know what you intend to study and how you intend to study it. The reader wants to know why your proposed study promises to be of importance or significance. The reader wants to know how your study fits into other work about the topic.

Such factors become the standards by which many graduate faculty judge a proposal. Lacking a clear statement of purpose and plan, it becomes difficult for others to evaluate what it is that you wish to do. More important,

> **Tip**
>
> Please recognize that your study must be approved by a committee of faculty. So, even though it is your study, you are not an autonomous actor. Often, these faculty members expect to see the conventional sections of the dissertation, and they expect to find these sections clearly labeled and accessible.

if you have not addressed the issues represented by the conventional
pieces of the proposal framework, it is possible that you will not have
a clear idea of what you want to do or how you want to do it. Lacking
such an understanding can cause you no small degree of anguish.

Parts of the Dissertation

A doctoral dissertation normally contains the following sections
or components:

Conventions in the Structure of the Dissertation

1. A Title Page

2. A Signature Page

3. An Abstract

4. An Acknowledgment Page

5. A Table of Contents

6. Lists of Tables, Graphs, and Figures

7. Chapter One: Background and Purpose and Research
   Questions and Significance

8. Chapter Two: A Review of the Literature

9. Chapter Three: Research Method

10. Chapter Four: Results and Analysis

11. Chapter Five: Conclusion and Recommendations

12. Citations

13. Appendices

Doctoral dissertations do not always include all of these
conventional sections. For various reasons, the doctoral researcher
may deviate from the patterns suggested by convention. However,
the researcher is well advised to understand the conventions covered
in this book and to have careful reasons for structuring his or her
study in a different way.

For example, it would be a rare dissertation in education and the social sciences that does not spring from a set of research questions. It would be a rare dissertation that has no purpose. It would be a rare dissertation that has no set procedure for laying out the process for gathering information or data. Each of the sections or chapters in a dissertation has subsets that many faculty members commonly expect to be included. And faculty members have good reasons for insisting on these conventions. In part, they serve to help the student through the stages of building a research study. In part, they serve to ensure that the study has a reasonable probability of advancing knowledge. For the nontraditional student, these conventions serve as a concrete guide.

There is a stylized quality to the dissertation. Most dissertation proposals contain an introductory section that includes a problem statement, a purpose statement, the research questions, a summary of the intended study, and a statement about the significance of the study. Following this introduction, typically labeled Chapter One, is a section that may offer historical information and a review of the scholarly literature about the topic. This section is typically labeled Chapter Two and is commonly referred to as the literature review. A third section or chapter describes the methodology that will be used to answer the research question(s). If a dissertation proposal is required as a first step, it is common that these first three sections constitute the proposal. Not infrequently, these three chapters are incomplete at the time the proposal is presented to the supervisory committee and become more elaborate as the dissertation itself is completed.

Title Page

A title should be fully explanatory when standing alone.

—Publication Manual of the APA, p. 11

Conventions abound. Your institution likely follows a set format for the title page; make sure you know this format. Take note of how other students have laid out the title pages of their published studies. Be careful with your title. Make sure it captures your study. Make sure it does not mislead. In many ways, the title is a shortcut to understanding the essence of your study. When you have completed your proposal, recheck your title. Does it stand alone as the representation of your work?

The Abstract

I keep six honest serving men. They taught me all I know; their
names are what and why and when and how and where and who.

—Rudyard Kipling*

When you read scholarly articles in search of information about your topic, you will usually find an abstract that summarizes the content, method, and findings of the article. The abstract is a convention in scholarly writing. It should be placed after the title page, before the table of contents. When your study is completed, it will be your abstract that conveys essential information to potential readers. The abstract should convey what you studied, why you studied it, how you studied it, what you found out, and what recommendations you make based on your analysis. Realize that the abstract of your study will appear in *Dissertation Abstracts* and will represent your dissertation in the public record. Realize also that you must convey everything about your study in 350 words or less. That constraint is unlikely to change. Future scholars interested in your topic will determine from your abstract whether or not they wish to explore your work more thoroughly.

On the following pages, I present two examples of abstracts. The first, written by Larry Cuban, is an example of a study that we would now label a multiple-case study. Cuban's abstract serves us as an exemplar in several ways. The purpose of the study is outlined. The process of the study is made clear. The findings are reported. Furthermore, if you search *Dissertation Abstracts* online for this study, you will find the bibliographic citation, but you will not find a text version of the abstract itself. You will still need to go to the library and look in the hard-bound copies of *Dissertation Abstracts* as the texts of abstracts appear only after 1980. This is an important piece of information for the nontraditional student. But, research libraries will help you locate the texts of abstracts in those studies done prior to 1980. In addition, if you were to do a word count, you would find Cuban's abstract exceeds the 350-word limit imposed today.

Example of an Abstract

SCHOOL CHIEFS UNDER FIRE:
A STUDY OF THREE BIG-CITY
SUPERINTENDENTS UNDER OUTSIDE PRESSURE

Cuban, Larry, Ph.D.

Stanford University, 1974

The issue of big-city superintendents under intense pressure is the subject of this study. Two broad questions guided this investigation. First, how did big-city school chiefs respond to outside pressure? Second, why did they respond the way they did? To narrow these questions to manageable proportions, three veteran urban schoolmen, highly respected by their colleagues, were examined. Carl Hansen of Washington, D.C., Benjamin C. Willis of Chicago, and Harold Spears of San Francisco came under intense pressure from groups outside the school system in the 1960s. In each city, two critical incidents that mirrored the conflict between each of these superintendents and external groups were investigated.

In Chicago, Willis faced and responded to charges of school segregation and the furor over an external evaluation of the school system. In San Francisco, Spears confronted a fracas over curriculum triggered by Sputnik and a concerted effort to end de facto school segregation. And in Washington, Hansen responded to a federally-funded effort to alter the school system as well as sharp pressure to desegregate schools that had become increasingly racially isolated.

What emerged from these three case studies was a similar response from the three schoolmen. While the cities differed in political cultures, school systems varied in size, and the three men were dissimilar in style, these three administrators normally expressed similar beliefs and pursued similar strategies in responding to outside pressure. Thus the second question: how to explain the mostly similar response pattern.

(Continued)

(Continued)

In approaching this question, two methods were used. First, there was an historical analysis of the writings and actions of urban superintendents over the last century. Second, various social science models of explanation were used. Theoretical models were built to interpret the context, meaning and direction of what the schoolmen perceived and did. Both approaches produced similar answers to the same question.

Three interacting contexts were uncovered. First, there was the historical residue of beliefs and practices that developed within the urban superintendency. Over the last century a series of "rights" and "wrongs" developed around the top posts. Refined and polished by experience, these norms formed the core of a professional ideology firmly embedded in historical experience.

Second, these superintendents experienced double socialization within the institution of the school. Initially as a student and later as a teacher, principal and central office administrator, the three schoolmen learned the norms, role demands, and expectations of the organization.

Finally, the nature of the school system as an organization generated conflicting demands upon their role as superintendent.

Three interacting contexts helped to explain why the schoolmen responded as they did. None of this, however, is to argue that school chiefs were wholly programmed by experience and circumstances to play out moves that were pre-ordained. Environmental factors, personal style and leadership role counted. The case studies clearly document each of these elements and the substantive influence on the course of events that each had.

Yet, the study does point to the limits of superintendent leadership in big cities. What is suggested is that large, urban schoolmen are not men of all seasons. Respected professionals to friends and stubborn bureaucrats to critics, Hansen, Willis, and Spears could not easily adjust to seasonal changes. The fit between the times they operated within, the political context and the dominant leadership conception each held seem to have greatly influenced their fortunes as school leaders.

Order No. 74-27,003, 282 pages.

Example of an Abstract

WOMEN MENTORING WOMEN: A PHENOMENOLOGICAL STUDY

Author(s): FITZPATRICK, JACQUELINE JACHYM

Degree: ED.D.

Year: 1996

Pages: 00180

Institution: UNIVERSITY OF SAN DIEGO; 6260

Advisor: MARY JO ABASCAL-HILDEBRAND

Source: DAI, 57, no. 04A, (1996): 1437

Abstract:

The purpose of this study was to examine the lived experience of ten business and professional women who have experienced a mentoring relationship as a mentor or protegee with another woman, to understand the essence of their mentoring experience, and to know more about their participation as mentors. This study began with the assumption that women who experienced mentoring whether from women or men would be active mentors themselves. However, the data reveal an important contradiction.

Since women are entering the business and professional ranks of the work force at an increasing pace, there are greater numbers of women who have reached positions of influence and are in situations to mentor other women. Likewise, there is also an increase in the number of women entering professions who may benefit from a mentoring relationship, especially as it concerns their workplace satisfaction and professional development. Thus, those who promote mentoring need to know more about its practice.

This qualitative study took a phenomenological approach to examine mentoring experiences; the data were collected during conversations that developed into narratives. This approach enabled these women participants to reflect deeply on their own mentoring experiences, and to consider how they in turn mentor others.

These women narrated their mentoring experiences as they examined the influences of family, education, and gender, as well

(Continued)

(Continued)

as their work. Part of this examination considered the historical context which has otherwise been repressive to women's development in general and to their career development in particular for these women aged thirty-eight to fifty-seven.

There are two major implications of this study. First, while these women are interested in mentoring, participate in and enjoy mentoring, and recognize the benefits of mentoring, they lack a commitment to specifically mentor other women. Second, this phenomenological methodology promoted their understanding about the way they seem to distance themselves from mentoring even though they believe they benefited from their own mentoring experiences.

SUBJECT(S)

Descriptor:

EDUCATION, ADULT AND CONTINUING

WOMEN'S STUDIES

Accession No:

AAG9626165

Note that in this abstract, which is more recent than the Cuban abstract, more information is available. For example, the advisor and the institutional affiliation are recorded. And, most significant, the text of the abstract is available online.

You may or may not wish to include an incomplete abstract of your study in your proposal. But, you will be asked to include an abstract at the conclusion of your work. Members of your committee will look for it, and they will expect it to convey what you studied, why you studied it, how you studied it, what you found out, and what you recommend.

The First Chapter

To have his path made clear for him is the aspiration of every human being in our beclouded and tempestuous existence.

—Joseph Conrad*

The first section or chapter of the proposal needs to convey to the reader the following information. Normally, one presents this information in separate sections. Many supervisory committee members look for some of these sections, particularly a purpose statement and a section on research questions, as they begin to read a proposal or dissertation:

1. The purpose of the study

2. The context or problem addressed in the study

3. The research question or questions

4. The general data-gathering method that will be employed

5. A list and definitions of technical terminology

6. Assumptions, delimitations, and limitations of the study

7. The significance of the study

Problem or Introductory Statement

The most important sentence in any article is the first one. If it doesn't induce the reader to proceed to the second sentence, your article is dead.

—Zinsser, 1990, p. 65

In constructing a dissertation, it is always helpful to be mindful of the nature of the task at hand. You are writing for an audience of faculty members. You are also writing for a wider peer community of fellow researchers and practitioners. The proposal is mainly for the first audience, the supervisory committee. Hence, there is a need to be economical and pragmatic. It is a good idea to define for your committee the research issue that you seek to inform. Identifying the nature of the problem has rhetorical power as well. The suggestion that Zinsser has in the quote above is important for you to remember. Pay attention not only to the content of your introductory statements but also to the form of these statements. If the problem is well stated and clearly of import, then this section will lend authority to your purpose.

Problems abound in education and the social sciences. What can be done to improve teaching? What causes desired change in some organizations and not in others? What happens to juvenile wards of a state when they never have a stable home life? The list of problems arising from practice seems endless. When, for example, special education moved toward *inclusion* as a classroom practice, a swarm of doctoral studies emerged to examine different obstacles to the pure goals of inclusion. Implicit in most of these studies was the belief or ideology that inclusion was the right thing to do. One problem quickly discovered by the special education research community was that the school system and its personnel were not aligned to implement inclusion. Because so many dissertations are grounded in problems of practice, it has become conventional to begin with the problem statement.

Below are several examples of problem statements. None of these are reported in totality.

Examples of Problem Statements

Many researchers recognize that involving parents in their child's education is an important way that teachers can influence parent perceptions of classroom/school climate and student progress (Aronson, 1986; Galinsky, 1989; and Greenwood & Hickman, 1991). Aronson discovered that many parents feel school staff are cool and indifferent toward them.

Stattelman, 1999

Social interaction in distance education traditionally described a process between the student and instructor that was mediated via correspondence. Using today's technological innovations, off-campus programming has a wider variety of methods at its disposal. One method, satellite delivery, is gaining interest. The popular "one-way video two-way audio" interactive system comes close to replicating a real classroom environment for the off-campus student including the availability for increased social action. It is unclear if the availability of increased classroom social interaction will be seen as a positive or negative influence in the life of the student

Burkhard-Kriesel, 1992

Since the fall of communism, and as more information becomes available to the West, it has become evident that a

(Continued)

(Continued)

social science infrastructure is lacking in the country of Romania. As a result, programs that seek to educate and strengthen families are needed but not found.

Asay, 1998

Controversy exists within the nursing profession concerning entry level nursing educational requirements for licensure as a registered nurse. Because graduates of all three programs (diploma, associate, and baccalaureate) must pass the same test for licensure, this study was conducted to determine whether program type significantly impacted entry level competence.

Hawkins, 2000

Dissertation problems are not limited to problems of practice. There may be a problem with a theoretical construction that stops short of explaining a phenomenon. When James Coleman undertook his famous study of student achievement and inequality, the relative contribution of family background to models of student achievement was not well understood. Thus, Coleman began with a theoretical problem: what measurable factors contribute most to variation in student achievement.

If you do begin this introductory chapter with a problem statement, remember that your reader also wants to know what you propose to do. Thus, don't go on for pages and pages about the problem. If necessary, you can have a longer background or context statement after you have introduced the purpose of your study.

Purpose Statement

You have your purpose well in mind when you can draft a critical, clear, and concise sentence that begins, "The purpose of this study is. . . ."

—Harry Wolcott, 1990

Sometimes dissertation writers elect to begin their introductory chapter with the purpose statement. Such a beginning is direct and to the point and helpful to the members of the supervisory committee. Proposals sometimes combine the problem statement and the purpose statement within the same section. This is usually acceptable and often is a more economical way of grounding your study in a context.

Begin the purpose statement with a declarative sentence. *This study will analyze or study or explore or be about. . . .* In the final draft of your completed dissertation, you will want to change the verb tense from the future to the past. *This study analyzed or explored or examined. . . .* This section need not be lengthy. In fact, a paragraph or two is sufficient. If you wish to reference the type of methodology you will use in this section, that is fine. Below are two examples of short declarative sentences containing a purpose statement.

Examples of Purpose Statements

This qualitative study will examine the education of early childhood educators in order to examine their familiarity with children's language development.

Shaunessey, 2001

The purpose of this study, using the naturalistic inquiry paradigm, will be to describe the experience of nursing staff during the process of Chief of Nursing Officer turnover and to discover success-oriented human resource interventions that facilitated the transition.

Bleich, 1997

It is best to keep the purpose statement short, direct, and to the point.

Context/Background

Most of us spend too much time on the last twenty-four hours and too little on the last six thousand years.

—Will Durant*

If the content of this section will simply repeat what has been written in the problem statement or purpose statement, this section should be omitted. Try always to avoid repeating the same material. Redundancy is too common in dissertations and distracts the reader when it is present. Often students elect to situate their study within the broad movements in their area of expertise. The 1983 report about

U.S. education, *A Nation at Risk,* has probably been cited more in the background section by students of educational administration studying educational reform than a person would care to count, or read for that matter. If your study is thoroughly grounded in a research tradition that will be well covered in a traditional literature review (the second chapter of your study), there is no need to cover that context in this section. You might elect to keep the context/background section brief or even exclude it.

If your study is about a problem in education, you may wish to expand beyond what was covered in a problem statement. If, for example, you are exploring a topic related to teacher retention, it would be quite appropriate to discuss in broad detail the difficulties that school districts experience in hiring and retaining particular types of teachers and include in that discussion relevant statistics that capture the problems with retention.

This context/background section may be a lengthy section, it may be brief, or it may be omitted. At some point, however, you do need to ground your study in the larger context. Below is an example of how one might attempt to ground a planned study of school effectiveness.

Examples of Grounding Study in Larger Context

When the American urban public school was confronted with huge numbers of new immigrant children at the turn of the nineteenth century, significant organizational ingenuity was needed. Sheer numbers meant that the earlier teaching of the young in small classrooms with genteel teachers had to give way to a structure that could process many children with many different skill levels. The result was the school district structure of the twentieth century. This was a hierarchical structure with a superintendent of schools and school board in charge. School became business-like (Tyack, 1974). As a result, those who study school organization have spent generations seeking ways to make the school organization more effective. In *Dissertation Abstracts*, a search under the search keywords "school" "district" "organization" and "effectiveness" uncovered 153 dissertations on this topic.

McLellan, 2002

I cite this example because it contains a very useful and informative strategy. The author turned to a searchable database, *Dissertation Abstracts*, in order to provide evidence of the sheer volume of research about the topic of school district effectiveness. Any scholar can do this. You can locate the total numbers of dissertations done on your topic by year or by decade. Thus, you can chart the waxing and waning interest in your topic. Below is an example using the search terms "teacher evaluation" to chart the interest in this topic by doctoral students over time.

Number of Dissertations about Teacher Evaluation		
1931–1940	=	5
1941–1950	=	21
1951–1960	=	104
1961–1970	=	217
1971–1980	=	810
1981–1990	=	2618
1991–2000	=	2294
Total	=	6069

Source: *Dissertation Abstracts*

Presenting data of this sort in a background/context section is one way to demonstrate that your topic has attracted the attention of the educational research community. Of course, the reverse can also be useful. If you search a database like *Dissertation Abstracts* and discover virtually no work on your particular topic, this type of evidence might lend credence to the necessity of your study. Or, such evidence might cause you to reconsider the significance of your study. Locating such information in the context or background statement provides an indication of how your topic fits into the current context of issues in your field.

Theoretical Base

An idea is a feat of association, and the height of it is a good metaphor.

—Robert Frost*

Not all advisors and supervisory committees expect to see a separate section in Chapter One labeled "theory" or "theoretical base." They expect to find the theoretical grounding for the study in the literature review. Sometimes your professors do not expect your study to be guided by theory. I include this section because theory can be, and usually is, a very important building block for a dissertation. If you have not done so, I encourage you to skim over the earlier section that discusses the place of theory. And if theory forms an important foundation for your research question, include a short section in Chapter One that presents this theoretical base.

As an aside, a number of reviewers for national research associations expect research proposals to include a section on the theory that guides the proposed study. For example, the inclusion of a section on the theoretical base of the study improves the odds that research proposals submitted to the scholarly divisions of the American Educational Research Association will be accepted.

Research Questions

The simplest questions are the hardest to answer.

—Northrup Frye*

The most difficult part of building the dissertation may well be the construction of the research question(s). The research question orients everything you do. If it is not clear and direct, your study will lose focus. The research question is your guide to what data you seek and to what data you select as important. When Nobel laureate Herbert Simon explored the human capacity for absorbing information, he coined the term *bounded rationality*. The term means that while we are bombarded with enormous amounts of information each waking moment, we have a limited capacity to process all that information. This bombardment of information or data quickly becomes one of the difficult problems of the dissertation researcher. The volume of writing about the topic may be huge. The amount of qualitative text may be absolutely overwhelming. The number of possible relationships in a quasi-experimental model may seem endless. The best way to manage such excess is with a good research question or set of research questions. Armed with such questions, you have a means of making all the decisions you must make about what to look for, what to exclude, what to emphasize, and what to discard. Armed with pointed research questions, your dissertation can be organized from start to finish with a clear focus.

Because the question and the method are entwined, there are differences between quantitative and qualitative questions. You would be wise to read carefully books covering the fine points of setting forth quantitative or qualitative research questions. It is customary for a student to present a necessary elaboration of research questions in a separate section on research method (Chapter Three in most dissertations). However, in Chapter One the researcher should simply state the research questions without much elaboration.

Furthermore, because the crafting of the research question(s) is so critical and so difficult, it has become conventional over time to identify the question(s) early in Chapter One. Advisors and committee members frequently turn to this section of the study right after they have read about the purpose of the study. For the faculty reader, the research question is a shortcut to the essence of the study. Therefore, it is important that great care be taken to make sure the question (1) is precise, (2) covers exactly the issue you wish to address, and (3) indicates how you will create your answer.

One way to better understand the research question is to look at what others have done. A number of books on research methods can provide you with examples. Refer specifically to Creswell (1994) and Piantanida and Garman (1999). Below are several examples of research questions from dissertation proposals or completed dissertations.

Questions From Quantitative Dissertations

Questions intended to be answered using quantitative data and statistical tests must be specific and detailed. The usual wording identifies both the issue to be addressed and the statistical mechanism that will be used to answer the question(s). Here are two questions from a study of Korean school administrators and their leadership attributes.

Examples of Quantitative Questions

1. To what degree do Korean principals subscribe to Confucian beliefs as measured by the Chinese Values Survey?

2. Do Korean principals report adhering to an authoritative leadership style as measured by the Leadership Scale?

Son, 2000

The phrase "To what degree" is characteristic of quantitative questions. "How much" is another. Usually the researcher will be measuring a relationship between a dependent variable(s) and independent variable(s). If you are developing a quantitative dissertation, you will wish to make patently obvious the relationship between dependent and independent variables. The two questions below delineate a clear relationship with leadership behaviors as a dependent variable and factors of emotional intelligence as independent variables.

Examples of Quantitative Questions

1. Is there a relationship between the total emotional intelligence and leadership behaviors of first-year department chairs as measured by the MSCEIT and LPI?

2. Is there a relationship between each of the subscales of emotional intelligence and leadership behaviors of first-year department chairs as measured by the MSCEIT and LPI?

Burbach, 2002

Your literature review should provide support for your claim about relationships. That is, other scholars who have studied the phenomena you study may well have explored how various factors relate to your dependent variable.

The research questions in the above examples are common in studies that use various types of instruments to measure dependent and independent variables. But, these questions are not as detailed as some advisors like. There is no mention of the statistical test and no indication of the conditions under which a finding of a difference or of no difference will be accepted. Some advisors supervising a student carrying out a quantitative study will want the research question to be expressed as the testing of a null hypothesis and will want confidence levels contained in the question for rejecting such a null hypothesis. If you are unclear about framing research questions as tests of the null hypotheses, you can find examples of this in

Tip

If you are using a quantitative research method with which your advisor is not familiar (logistic regression possibly), make sure you have careful advice from someone who is familiar with your research technique. Make sure your research question is compatible with your quantitative design.

most research textbooks. As indicated earlier, the researcher usually provides for a fuller elaboration of the details of the research method and questions in a separate Chapter Three.

Qualitative Questions

The common format for the qualitative study is to ask a broad and all-encompassing question. Some call this the *grand tour* question. Such a broad question is useful because typically the qualitative researcher does not want to be restricted by the question(s) of the study. Rather, the question needs to be liberating in the sense that it affords the researcher wide latitude to explore. Creswell wrote, "This question, consistent with the emerging methodology of qualitative designs, is posed as a general issue so as not to limit the inquiry" (1994, p. 79). There are growing numbers of specific qualitative methodologies, each with its own unique properties: case studies, phenomenology, grounded theory studies, and so on. But the format of research questions is similar across these various qualitative studies.

Consider the examples of qualitative questions presented below in Examples of Qualitative Questions From Proposals. The first set represents a common way of asking the overarching question the student wishes to address in the dissertation: How do _____ describe the _____? What meaning does _____ attribute to _____? As indicated above, sometimes such a question is labeled the grand tour question. To learn more about writing the qualitative research question, refer to books about qualitative research listed in the annotated bibliography, such as Wolcott or Marshall and Rossman. In addition, Rossman and Rallis (1998) and Piantanida and Garman (1999) both provide useful illustrations of qualitative questions. The big question serves a useful purpose. Intentionally broad and encompassing, such a question affords the researcher wide latitude to explore where her or his data lead.

The typical question, "how do" or "how does such and such experience a phenomenon," can be construed as awkward when given a literal interpretation. If you want to know how I experience the process of creating a backyard garden, I may tell you simply that I do so by digging one. You, on the other hand, may want to know what value or worth I attribute to such an endeavor. If this is the case, then you want to ask me about my attributions of worth or my held beliefs about value. Make sure your questions guide you where you want to go.

Below are examples of descriptive qualitative questions. Implicit in such "how do" questions is the idea that these questions will elicit a wide range of qualitative data.

Examples of Qualitative Questions From Proposals

How do freshmen students describe the experiences of living in a residence hall learning community?

Buss, 2001

How do African American and Latino/a students on a predominantly white campus describe their organizational involvement experience?

Knudson, 1997

How do participants in the McNair Project at the University of Nebraska describe their experiences?

Eckstrom, 2000

How do teachers and staff at the T. J. Pappas School perceive the role that student/teacher relationships play in the educational process of children in their classroom?

Voelker, 2001

What is the experience of nursing staff during the interregnum following Chief Nursing Officer separation/turnover?

Bleich, 1997

What academic preparation is needed for college-level United States history students?

Wunder, 1994

What were the perceptions and understandings of Native American and Australian Aboriginal students concerning the cultural conflict which arises between their traditional beliefs, values and norms and their experiences of mainstream universities?

Cantrell, 1992

> ## Tip
>
> As you work on your question(s), get others involved in critiquing what you propose. Often what seems to be clear to us will be confusing to others. In addition, check carefully to see if your research question matches your purpose. Sometimes we discover to our dismay that our purpose is different from the questions we pose. A peer group can be very useful in this regard.

The above are common types of broad qualitative questions. In an additional resource, Creswell (1994) covers the topic of research questions in excellent detail and provides many examples of questions in quantitative and qualitative studies. Rossman and Rallis (1998) give useful examples of qualitative questions.

Your research questions serve as a guide. These questions serve as the rudder with which you steer the ship of your dissertation. Make sure the rudder is functioning.

Method

Plan your work and work your plan.

—Paul Bullock, Burr and Burton Academy,
personal communication, 1959

Often it helps briefly to identify the methodology you will use to examine your research questions as a short section in this introductory chapter. This need not be a long section, particularly if your study will use a quantitative methodology that will be fully developed in Chapter Three. In fact, dissertation convention reserves Chapter Three for the lengthier discussion of methodology. But, it helps your supervisory committee to be given a brief summary of your intended method. Such a short section is another example of how you can assist your committee in better understanding your study.

Example

The study will use the Delphi Technique in gathering data from subjects. The Delphi Technique has been used extensively to predict future technology, customer preferences, industry change, etc. Champers and Mullick (1979) described the technique as a "method for soliciting unbiased expert opinion and obtaining a consensus through a sequence of questionnaires utilizing controlled feedback."

Hamilton, 2002

Definition of Terms

President Reagan didn't always know what he knew.

—Lt. Col. Oliver North*

Dissertations are very focused research studies. By the word *focused* I mean that dissertations are specific, not general. Dissertations normally explore a very limited set of questions and usually contain language that is specific to the study. Dissertation authors thus will use terminology that may be misunderstood if one makes no effort to define the special terms in the study. Make sure that your reader knows what you know.

To do this, there is the convention of having a section devoted just to terminology. You define terms that have special meaning. Sometimes we utilize a specific word or phrase with a very precise meaning in mind. All professional jargon, technical language, and specific words and phrases that are important to the argument and meaning of the study should be presented in a list of terms. These definitions do not need to have been written by others, although they may have been. Often the definition will be found in the research literature. Sometimes you will coin your own special definition. To gain a sense of how dissertation writers define the terminology for their studies, browse through some dissertations. It is not necessary to define terms that will be commonly understood. Use common sense. Will a reader not particularly familiar with your subject understand the words you use?

Assumptions

Philosophy is nagging, it cajoles students into asking questions about basic assumptions, it generates doubts and uncertainties, and, it is said, it keeps people from getting their work done.

—Eisner, 1991, p. 4

Eisner goes on to point out that as researchers we must be concerned with the core concepts in social science inquiry that are, in fact, philosophical in nature: objectivity, validity, truth, fact, theory, structure (1991, p. 4). These concepts impact any research project. No research study is perfect in its design. Some are more persuasive or believable than others. None is perfectly accurate in its approach and its

> ### Tip
>
> In writing the sections of this first chapter, don't feel you have to complete each section before going on to the next section. If you have trouble with the research questions, work on the assumptions you will make or the context or the significance of your study. The important task is to keep writing until you have a workable draft of the chapter. Then share it with your advisor and with others willing to read it.

findings. That is, no study will answer its research questions with complete certainty. The reason for this imperfection lies in the assumptions that we all bring to our efforts to understand how and why things work the way they do.

We make assumptions about how research subjects will behave. Will they tell us the truth as they see it? Will they be forthright with us? Will they intentionally deceive us? We make assumptions about our own behavior. Will we ask the right questions? Will we gather the right kind of information in sufficient detail and amount? Will we, as the products of our own experiences, examine our data and information impartially? We make assumptions about the tools we use to gather and analyze data. That is, our chosen research method is predicated on epistemological assumptions about what constitutes legitimate knowledge and what constitute legitimate ways of acquiring that knowledge. If we do survey research, we make assumptions about the validity of our individual questions and how these questions will be understood by our subjects. If we do case studies, we make assumptions about whether the case that we have chosen really contains the information we seek. If we do statistical analyses, we make assumptions about the normal distribution of our data. In doing sampling, for example, a scholar will be gathering data from a limited number of subjects, usually at a single point in time. In order to generalize one's findings from this sample to a larger population, one must make assumptions about both the representativeness of the sample and about the stability of findings gathered at one point in time. Many factors can impact the stability of one's findings.

In short, all of our research projects spring from assumptions. These are not the theories that we may be exploring. Rather, they are the beliefs we bring to the study that we will accept as valid. The identification of these beliefs helps bring legitimacy to your role as a scholar. In this section, it is appropriate to attempt to identify some of the major assumptions that you bring to your study.

Example

The underlying assumption of this study was that the values that motivate chief development officers could be identified and understood utilizing the Spectrum I Test of Adult Work Motivation questionnaire. It was assumed that chief development officers participating in this study were responsible for the fund-raising program's success or lack of success. Additionally, endowment growth or decline was assumed to be reflective of the fund-raising success or failure at the institutions involved in the study.

Miller, 1991

Delimitations and Limitations

Just as it is important to identify assumptions, it is important to identify delimitations and limitations. If some future scholar should seek to replicate your study, your identification of the factors that make your study unique will be important for that future scholar. While she or he will likely be unable to replicate your study down to the last detail, what you write in this section will help others assess the quality of your study and possibly pattern future studies after what you have done.

Having said this about delimitations and limitations, I should also note that doctoral dissertation writers frequently have trouble with this section of their opening chapter. What do these two terms mean and how are they different? This is a frequent question.

Delimitations

Delimitations are the factors that prevent you from claiming that your findings are true for all people in all times and places. For the quantitative study, these are the factors that limit generalization. For the qualitative study, these are the factors that limit the relevancy of your study to other populations or individuals. If I study only the nurses of Oregon, I will not be able to extend my results to the nurses of Arkansas. If I study three adolescent Hispanic female students, I cannot claim that their experiences will necessarily parallel those of Sudanese students of the same age. Many quantitative studies gather data at a moment in time. Would your study arrive at a different conclusion if you were to gather data at a different point in time? Possibly. Such issues impose delimitations. A good resource identifying issues associated with design delimitations in quantitative studies is Campbell and Stanley's 1966 article on experimental and quasi-experimental designs for research in *Handbook of Research on Teaching*. It may help to think of a researcher 30 years from now who seeks to replicate your study. What factors may get in the way of an exact replication? These are delimitations. These are restrictions imposed by the design of your study.

Example

A delimitation of this study is that the unit of analysis will be confined to executives who orchestrated or managed the turnover event and those persons who had experienced the departure of a chief nursing officer. The organizational structures, the scope of job responsibilities, and the number of departments that report to a chief nursing officer can vary dramatically between facilities. This study will not account for the reactions of all groups about the departure of a chief nursing officer.

Bleich, 1997

In the example above, the doctoral student points out that the study is designed to gather data on the impact of an administrator turnover from a select class of subjects. Thus, conclusions will be delimited in the sense that if a wider number of employees were included, the findings might differ.

Limitations

Now, think of your method. It will remain constant. That is, 30 years from now that researcher who wishes to replicate your study can do so using the same method. That future researcher using the same research method will face the same limitations you face. These have to do with the means you have chosen for gathering and analyzing data. Limitations are those restrictions created by your methodology. A survey always seeks to find ways to increase the return rate. An ethnography can only capture the experiences of those studied. A historiography will spring from the cultural and sociological context in which it is written. An analysis of variance requires that variables conform to an assumption of normal distribution. Limitations are the *built-in* limits of the method you use to explore your question. If you are thoughtful and analytical about your chosen method, you should have no difficulty identifying the design factors that might produce inaccurate or misleading data and possibly lead to mistaken conclusions.

Example

A limitation to this quasi-experimental design is that experimental groups, knowing that they are receiving training on customer service, may improve their service due to the Hawthorne effect and that effect may influence the performance based outcomes that were chosen to be measured.

DiPietro, 2002

Significance

This is a very important section of a proposal. It is the section where you answer the question: Why should anybody care about my study? In this section, you offer your reasons and arguments pertaining to why your study is important. These reasons may be confined to the potential that your study will add new knowledge to existing information about your area of interest; these reasons may relate to how practitioners behave and act in carrying out their work. This section is usually brief. A page or two should certainly suffice to lay out the potential significance of what you hope to add to the scholarly literature.

There is nothing wrong with a little humility. It is okay to suggest that your study may not have earth-altering consequences. But, your research community—the

Tip

I usually tell my own doctoral students to be cautious in admitting to any weakness. Don't downplay the potential importance of your study. One wants to be cognizant of weaknesses in design and method, but I think it is a strategic mistake to speak too loudly of weaknesses in concept or method until after the dissertation proposal has been approved. Then, in the final draft, it is appropriate to be reflective on what went wrong and what could have been done better. Acknowledge weaknesses in design, method, and execution. Such weaknesses will be there. But, assuming your study holds together, don't be so self-critical that others will end up doubting the efficacy of your study.

other scholars who study what you study—and your committee members will expect you to do a study that has the promise of making a contribution. This is the section in which you attempt to guess at that potential contribution.

Summary

Chapter 2 has presented you with a recipe. Now you know the main ingredients of the dissertation's introductory chapter. Paying attention to these as you develop your study will serve you well, accomplishing the following:

- You will have a clear statement of what you intend to do.
- You will have a question or set of questions that will guide your search for information.
- You will have a plan for gathering that information.
- You will have expectations for why your study has the potential of making a contribution to knowledge about your topic.
- You will be able to provide your advisor and supervisory committee with a coherent and understandable proposal.

As a nontraditional student, this presentation of the first chapter of a dissertation should help you as you work independently on one of the biggest challenges of your doctoral degree.

3

The Literature Review

Research is the process of going up alleys to see if they are blind.

—Marston Bates*

What is research but a blind date with knowledge.

—Will Henry*

This chapter covers the literature review and includes a detailed discussion of how to make the most efficient use of the research library using much improved search capabilities. It offers you a great deal of important information about one of the most demanding of dissertation conventions: an examination of the scholarly work that has explored your topic.

Conventions in the Literature Review

1. The student is expected to be an authority on the dissertation topic.

2. Research studies in which a scholar has gathered data or information and reported that data serve to ground the dissertation study or guide the interpretation of data.

(Continued)

(Continued)

3. The literature review is often presented in the second chapter of the dissertation, or in some qualitative studies, it is used to interpret qualitative findings in concluding chapters.

4. There is a standard way to report research literature.

5. The review is expected to cover research presented in scholarly journals, academic press publications, and dissertation abstracts.

The phrase *literature review* refers to that section of the dissertation in which one identifies and describes the scholarly studies that others have done about the topic of the dissertation. Faculty advisors generally expect that dissertations will be grounded in previous work of scholars. It is hard to make the claim that a dissertation is adding to existing knowledge if there is no assessment of that existing knowledge. Even in qualitative studies that seek to build new theory, knowledge of existing work is essential, for a person must know what exists before he or she can add to that knowledge.

Accessing and searching for information in a research library is an important part of this process. I include in this chapter a detailed description of how to make the most of a research library, orienting this discussion particularly for nontraditional students who must work at a distance. The design and construction of the literature review often poses a challenge for doctoral students since this proves to be a new experience for most. This challenge is not alleviated by the growing willingness of supervisory committees to be permissive about this dissertation convention. Wolcott wrote:

> Although chapter two is a favorite spot for the traditional literature review, there is no ironclad rule—even in the otherwise totally inflexible graduate school at my university—that chapter two *must* be a literature review. (Wolcott, 1990, p. 17)

Creswell added:

> Although I recommend placing the literature toward the end of the qualitative study (to be compared and contrasted with the outcomes of the study), it also can be found in the

introduction to "frame" the problem or in a separate section called the Review of the Literature. (Creswell, 1994, p. 37)

The expectations of the supervisory committee regarding the literature review are not always clear to the doctoral student.

Conventions speak to the literature review. First, you are supposed to be an authority on your topic. You can't be an authority if you don't know the scholarship that has been done on the topic. Second, you are expected to interpret your data in light of what others have found. Third, the convention is to have the second chapter of the dissertation contain the literature review. Check with your advisor before abandoning this convention. Fourth, realize you will want to use the literature about your topic as you interpret and analyze your data no matter the research tradition (quantitative or qualitative) from which you write.

> **Tip**
>
> It is wise to ask your advisor about the literature review early in the process of planning the study. Do this by phone, e-mail, or personal visit so that you gain some insight into this person's expectations of your study. Ask your advisor to recommend a dissertation that contains a particularly exemplary literature review.

Quantitative and Qualitative Literature Reviews

The methodological disputes between the quantitative and qualitative research traditions have resulted in different understandings about the use of the literature review. According to some authors of research methods texts, a literature review about a topic should not be used as a guide by the qualitative researcher. That is, the qualitative researcher has to be able to see with her or his own eyes and not be unduly influenced by what others have written. There is a certain logic to this argument. It is an argument that doctoral students sometimes use as a way of justifying why no literature review is needed. Beware of this position. Not all advisors agree with such an argument about the importance of the literature review in qualitative work. Fetterman offered a sensible dictum relative to the issue of the literature review in qualitative studies: "The ethnographer enters the field with an open mind, not an empty head" (1989, p. 11). By implication, any researcher, not just the ethnographer, needs to be well informed about his or her topic.

Literature Review

> *Getting more information is learning and so is coming to under-*
> *stand what you did not understand before. But there is an impor-*
> *tant difference between these two kinds of learning. To be*
> *informed is to know simply that something is the case. To be*
> *enlightened is to know, in addition, what it is all about: why it is*
> *the case, what its connections are with the other facts, in what*
> *respects it is the same, in what respects it is different, and so forth.*

—Adler & van Doren, 1972, p. 11

The quote above comes from a wise book by Adler and van Doren called *How to Read a Book.* In this book, the authors discuss two types of learning: (1) learning by instruction and (2) learning by discovery. In building your literature review, you are learning by discovery. And, as the quote implies, you should be enlightened as a result of this process. I want to emphasize this point. Your goal in conducting a literature review is to know what your topic is all about, why the forces that shape your topic have the impact they do, and how your topic fits in the larger scheme of events and matters. In this chapter, I share with you the many aspects of conducting a literature review about your topic. This chapter is offered under the assumption that your dissertation will contain a review of the literature.

Beginning a Literature Review

What research studies have been written about your topic? Is your topic widely researched? Have there been landmark studies? Who are the scholars in your area that have achieved prominence for their work? What do these scholars say about your topic? Is your intended study related to this previous research work? Who are the doctoral students who have studied your topic and what have they found out? How do you add to the previous work done by other scholars?

Conversely, are there but a few studies? Perhaps no person has studied what you wish to study. Are you able to demonstrate this? Can you say with certainty that your study is unique and has the promise of exploring a brand new area, and that, remarkably, no other scholar has studied what you wish to study? And if this is your claim, is your project of sufficient significance that it will be of value to the field?

The literature review provides the scholarly context for what you wish to do. The knowledge you gain from this exploration through the literature about your topic also helps you refine your own study and gives you an array of conceptual tools to help you design your study and to interpret your own data. The only way to provide this scholarly context is to search and to read.

Types of Research Material

> **Tip**
>
> Realize that if you choose to study a tiny subset of a population in a very specific setting, this does not mean you should neglect the research about your topic that may have been carried out for other populations in other settings. For example, studying the leadership behaviors of Hispanic men in small nonprofit organizations in a single county in a single state does not mean you do not need to inform your readers about leadership behaviors in nonprofit organizations generally and of Hispanic men in general.

There are many different types of research material for you to search in building your literature review. Remember that your study belongs as part of a larger research community. Who are the leaders in that community? How and where does that community display its work? Who takes note of the work done in this research community? What work is most important and how do you arrive at a judgment about importance? To address such questions with confidence, one casts a wide net. Below are the types of library resources that will help you to do so.

**Types of Research Resources
From the Publication Manual of the
American Psychological Association (APA)**

Journal Articles
Submitted Manuscripts
Government Documents
Magazine Articles
Monographs

(Continued)

(Continued)

Newspaper Articles
Books
Book Chapters
In-press Books
Technical Reports
Proceedings of Meetings and Symposia
Doctoral Dissertations and Master's Theses
Unpublished Work
Book Reviews
Audiovisual Material
Electronic Media

Below I cover the types of material most commonly presented in literature reviews.

Primary Sources

In constructing a literature review, it is important to locate primary sources, that is, the actual reports of research. Often, textbooks or general-interest publications refer to work done by others. It is the work done by these others that forms the primary sources. Thus, it is said that Carol Gilligan learned by looking at primary sources (in her case, the actual research reports of Kohlberg) that in developing his theories of human moral development, Kohlberg used male subjects. This led her to ask if the experiences of girls would be comparable to boys (Gilligan, 1982). Her work led her to conclude that girls experience different stages of moral development than those advanced in Kohlberg's work. It is possible that had she not read Kohlberg's research reports, she would not have been aware of the true nature of his population base. The annals of research are full of examples where the examination of earlier scholarship has led to exciting new studies.

The primary resources are the writings of those doing the research and scholarship, not the writings of those who describe these original scholars.

Where do you find this work? Those who report their research typically do so in professional journals. Most fields have such journals. In education, professional journals abound. These are distinguished from more popular magazines because the work published in these journals must be screened by means of an external review. That is, when a scholar sends a research report to the journal, the editor then submits the work to other scholars in the field, requesting their judgments as to the quality and validity of the proposed article. Depending on the judgments of this external review, the editor may or may not elect to publish the work. This practice leads to the term *refereed article.* In the top journals in a field, there are many more submissions than an editor can publish, so competition for recognition in such journals is keen. Major research libraries carry a wide array of journals, although budget cuts have reduced numbers in recent years. These are the types of journals that should contain the reports of research that may inform your study.

Research organizations like the RAND Corporation and the American Institutes for Research often produce detailed studies. These are sources that can contain a great deal of information based on collected data. Scholars at the American Institutes for Research, for example, recently completed a large-scale study of the impact of the California initiative to reduce class size in schools and thereby increase student achievement.

Dissertation Abstracts

Another main source for primary research about your topic is *Dissertation Abstracts.* The abstracts of virtually all doctoral dissertations published at universities in the United States are collected and published by *Dissertation Abstracts.* These are now made available to research libraries as electronic databases, easily searchable and readily accessible. Virtually all research libraries subscribe to this database.

In *Dissertation Abstracts,* you can search by key word, by subject area, by author, or by your advisor's name (always a wise thing for a doctoral student to do). You can also search to see what dissertations your committee members have supervised (another wise thing for a doctoral student to do). Check the drop-down menu to locate the variety of ways you can search this database. Note, also, that if using *Dissertation Abstracts,* you can e-mail copies of abstracts and citations to your e-mail address. This is a very useful way for you to manage the accumulation of citations that occurs as you conduct your literature review. It is wise to create folders in which you can store e-mails that pertain to particular topics. This also is a useful way of managing information that will build exponentially as you conduct your search.

> **Tip**
>
> Don't wait. Log in to *Dissertation Abstracts*. See what this database can do for you. Search for studies that are of interest and read the abstracts.

There is no reason not to do a careful search of these abstracts to determine if other dissertations have dealt with material similar to yours. Furthermore, when you locate relevant studies, the literature review conducted in such a study can provide you with good leads to other relevant research.

Once you discover dissertations that appear to be relevant to your topic, you have several options. Your library may be able to secure a copy of the dissertation for you through interlibrary loan. Or, you can order your own copies of these studies for a price through your library. These can also be ordered directly from *Dissertation Abstracts* online. This service is currently being provided by ProQuest. Search online for *Dissertation Abstracts*. Below is a recent price list in U.S. dollars.

Ordering Dissertations and Theses

Price List

	Microfilm Paper	Softcover Paper	Hardcover Express (Unbound Paper)	Dissertation
Academic	$39.00	$43.00	$53.00	$34.00
Nonacademic	$53.00	$63.00	$77.00	$34.00
International	$53.00	$63.00	$77.00	$37.00, Express $55.00

* 2003 Price List

Many faculty members expect that you will cite dissertations in conducting your own study. Be alert to this expectation.

Reviews of Research

Some of the best shortcuts for the student seeking to identify the important research about a topic are articles that do just that: these articles summarize the important work about a topic. In the field of education, there are several important reviews that may serve as a gold mine for the dissertation scholar. The *Review of Research in Education* has been produced by the American Educational Research Association (AERA) for years and is an excellent source. The same association also publishes two journals, the *American Educational Research Journal* and the *Educational Researcher,* that often contain literature reviews. The National Society for the Study of Education also produces annual volumes that contain reviews of important topics. Such sources can serve a scholar well.

Example

Local school boards have traditionally governed public education in the United States but have seldom been the focus of empirical research. This article provides a review of literature published in the past two decades on the role and effectiveness of local school boards, specifically with respect to school boards' influence on students' academic achievement.

Land, 2002

Secondary Sources

In addition to those who do the research and report the results of their study, many scholars write about the work of the primary scholars. These writings, labeled secondary sources, can provide very useful contextual information for you and can often help you place in context the more detailed and focused work of the primary scholars. Textbooks, theme works, and special editions are examples of secondary sources. Books on a topic are important secondary sources. If, for example, you were interested in how learners react to different forms of external and internal motivation, Alfie Kohn's book *Punished by Rewards* would serve as an invaluable resource (Kohn, 1999). If you wanted to learn about the school superintendent and his or her relationship with a school board, Land's review of research on local school boards would be important (Land, 2002).

A wealth of information can be found in the various publications that national educational associations produce on various topics. The federal government and state governments also publish many reports that can be useful. The federal government in particular has produced scores of such reports on particular topics; the government documents section of your research library should not be overlooked.

Popular Press Sources

There are many journals and magazines devoted to educational and social science topics. National magazines serve as a timely resource as do large newspapers. Material from these sources is relevant to your study but should not be substituted for the primary research upon which these opinion and journalistic pieces are based. An article on college dropouts published in *Newsweek* magazine or the *Washington Post* may provide you with a sound citation to support a point. The conclusions made in such articles, however, are normally not the result of a systematic collection of information.

Social Science Citation Index

This electronic database is now provided through ISI Web of Knowledge, more familiarly known as Web of Science, a vendor that maintains this index and two others—the Science Citation Index Expanded and the Arts and Humanities Citation Index. Because this database is quite expensive, not all libraries subscribe to it. It is a very useful tool, however, and if your library has it, you will want to track the major figures of your research community through this database.

> ISI Web of Knowledge is an integrated platform designed to support research in academic, corporate, government, and not-for-profit organizations.

At the end of a research article, it is common for the author to provide a list of other researchers that have been cited in the text of the article. Imagine how useful it would be if you could track the times and places in which an author had been cited by others. Such information would allow you to identify others who found the work of a particular scholar germane. You could thus expand your knowledge of others doing research on your topic. You could also determine who has become a prominent scholar on your topic by virtue of the frequency with which others cite her or him.

The Social Science Citation Index does this. You can search by subject term, by author name, by journal title, or by author affiliation. You can search for articles that cite an author or an article that you specify. It tracks the citations from a selected list of journals (over 1,725 journals), indexes these citations (averages 2,500 new records per week), and publishes a yearly record of that index (contains a total of over 3.15 million records). It is not a database to be neglected.

Conference Sources

Most disciplines have major conferences at which scholars present their research. Sometimes the proceedings of such conferences are published. These can be very valuable sources of current work. In education, the largest and most well-attended international conference is that of the AERA. The proceedings of this conference are now available on the association's Web site. If you do not know the identity of the professional associations that hold conferences in your area of interest, you need to find that out.

Then, as a potential source of research about your topic, you need to explore the presentations that have been made at these annual meetings.

> **Tip**
>
> Ask your advisor about professional meetings that you should monitor. Find out where your advisor thinks you might be able to present your doctoral study once it is completed.

Internet Sources

Internet sources are becoming more important to the literature review, especially as online journals grow in number. In some instances, you will find individuals self-publishing their work. Many scholars now have their own Web sites. In some instances, you will find Web sites of direct relevance to the topic you are studying. Many funded research projects develop Web sites as a vehicle for disseminating their research. I offer more information about the Internet later in this chapter.

Publishing Houses

In recent years, many publishing companies have emerged that focus on particular disciplinary areas. A number of them, especially university presses, concentrate on the field of education. One excellent resource you may wish to use to identify these publishers can be found in the list of exhibitors that appears in the conference schedule of national associations. The conference bulletin of the AERA contains a long list of publishers who focus on educational work.

The above constitutes a list of potential areas of scholarly activity in which you should be able to find information about your topic. Remember, you are mainly looking for scholarship that has gathered data about your topic and presented it in an objective manner. Now I turn to how to treat the research once you have found it.

Conduct of the Review

Conventions guide the manner in which you behave as a scholar in reporting research. These conventions include ethical as well as practical behaviors.

Academic Rigor

One of the questions that frequently comes from doctoral students in dissertation proposal classes is whether it is permissible to cite a source they have not read or have gleaned from someone else. This issue is of true relevance for the nontraditional student simply because there will be a constraint on the amount of time such a student can devote to reading library material. Note that we are discussing research reporting here, not journalistic pieces in a news-paper or popular press. If another author appears to have done a thorough and factual job discussing a piece of relevant research, is it wrong to accept that author's judgment and also quote the piece of relevant research without inspecting it first hand? The first answer is yes, it is wrong. How can you know that the conclusions of the research project you wish to report are accurately summarized unless you look for yourself? History is constantly being reunderstood as new generations revisit the scholarship of earlier decades. The same phenomenon is true of doctoral research. Hence, you may bring a very different perspective to a past interpretation of data.

The second answer is that researchers commonly do cite work by relying on the reporting of others. I believe this practice as evidenced in the dissertation literature review has become more common because doctoral students are more part time and more distant. To read every piece of work about a dissertation topic might, depending on the nature of the dissertation topic, require months in a research library. Since many nontraditional doctoral students are unable to devote that amount of time to reading, there is a growing tendency to rely on the reporting of others.

The downside of this practice is that one may endorse poor research that should not be accentuated. The annals of scholarship are full of deflated research projects that fail tests of replication. The Piltdown Man turned out to be a hoax. So did the Piltdown chicken. Scientists Pons and Fleschmann thought they had invented a cold fusion process only to have their findings discredited. And we may not know the color of the universe but we do know it is not turquoise. Science in all disciplines is full of conclusions that have not been or cannot be substantiated. Stephen Jay Gould took years of delight in tracking the scholarly follies of researchers. Thus, one needs to be wary of accepting the conclusions of others about the veracity and rigor of research.

Still, to adopt a standard that says no work shall be reported unless it has been read would be a difficult standard for any doctoral student. I venture to guess it would be difficult to find a completed doctoral dissertation in which the author could claim to have read every piece of research cited.

I have found an uneasy compromise. I tell the doctoral students with whom I work that they should read any study that is directly related to their dissertation topic. One should cite studies that are tangential to the direct focus of the dissertation or that fall into the category of related studies. But one may elect not to read all of these studies. If one cites but does not read the review by another scholar, one should have sufficient detail about the study being reported so that one feels comfortable including the study in question as part of her or his literature review. If the scholar simply says, "I or we found that *this and this* were true," but provides no information regarding method or subjects or research design, I would be wary of including it without reading the study. One does not want to report subjective opinion as if it were research. Shortly I provide a list of items that one should include in reporting research. If the scholar you wish to cite does not provide you with such information, be wary of accepting that scholar's conclusions and recommendations.

Scope of the Review

When do I stop? That is a question often asked. The more a person explores, the more she or he finds. Or at least, this is the common experience. Issues abound in how to organize an exponentially growing volume of literature. So, when is enough enough? Here are a few guidelines.

First, you certainly want to know the current thinking about your topic. Thus, you do not want to miss some work that is current and represents the mainstream views. Second, you want to be able to talk authoritatively about the research that has been done in your area. Third, when you notice that other scholars repeatedly cite research that you have already identified, you have probably mined the literature in your area. Fourth, when you are familiar with the names that others mention to you, you can begin to feel confident in the scope of your review.

Do not make assumptions about the literature that surrounds your topic. If you have cast about and found very little in the way of actual research activity, make sure that you validate your conclusion that little research exists with your advisor and committee. And make certain that you have not neglected a whole body of work that has been done under a different label. Truly unexplored fields of inquiry are rare in education and the social sciences.

Currency

How far back do I have to go in my literature review is an oft-asked question. The answer usually given is this: You are supposed to be an expert on the topic that you have chosen. You should know all of the important work that has been published. If there is a long historical trail of work that goes back decades into the past, report the work of the major scholars in that tradition. As noted elsewhere, beware of changes in nomenclature and labels. In many fields, the same phenomena may be represented by changes in labels.

At the same time, you are expected to be part of a scholarly community that is actively exploring a topic. Thus, unless there is a total dearth of research activity about your topic, you are expected to include up-to-date research in your review. If your review contains no citations of work in recent years, it is probable that you will be quizzed about this. For this reason, you always want to be diligent in searching relevant journals, conference proceedings, dissertation abstracts, and publishing houses.

Organizing and Writing the Literature Review

Assuming you are writing a chapter in your study about the research literature, begin with an organizer. Describe how you intend to present the literature.

Sometimes one organizes literature by topical areas, sometimes in chronological order. It can be very useful for you and your reader to have some kind of advanced organizer. Rudestam and Newton (1992) wrote, "The review of the literature is generally preceded by a brief introduction." Glatthorn (2002) suggested a description of the search process that you utilized as a useful way to begin your chapter of the literature review. Creswell (1994) has proposed a literature map or schematic that lays out the component parts of the literature review. All of these authors are after the same end: a convenient and clear picture or overview of this chapter's content that is presented at the beginning of the literature review.

You have several standard options to organize the work. One is to order your reporting in a chronological manner. Begin with the oldest research and work your way to the present, chronicling the tradition that surrounds your topic. A second is to begin with the seminal scholarship that has been most widely recognized as influential. A third way is to begin with the problem of practice that energized the research community. In each of these organizational formats, your literature review will be most easily tracked if you tell a story, a story of discovery and accomplishment. Most of what you will do in this literature review is report on what other scholars have done and found out. Make this story interesting. As Adler and van Doren implied in the quote earlier in this section, enlightenment is the goal.

Describing Research

In citing particular research articles, there is a common, stylized, and useful convention or way of writing about a research study. You should identify the researchers, tell what the researchers studied, describe how they studied the topic, indicate what results they found, and provide some critical comment about the validity or quality of the research design. Below are three examples of the typical way that research studies are presented. The first is a general and nonspecific review of what a particular scholar has concluded. The second is a review of a quantitative research study; the third is a review of a qualitative research study.

Example 1: General Review, Nonspecific

McComb's theory on "self-regulated learning and academic achievement, a phenomenological view" (In Zimmerman & Schunk, 1989), contributes to the body of literature related to adult learners. In her historical background on phenomenology she cited two early indigenous phenomenologists (sic) in America, Snygg and Combs, as being interested in self-awareness theories during the 1940s.

Sookram, 1996

Commentary: This is an example of reporting the general work of a scholar and not the particular research studies that undergird the work. It is general in nature and not specific.

Below is a more detailed report of a research project.

Example 2: Quantitative Dissertation Study

Using multiple regression, West (2002) examined the relationship of student achievement to a variety of school district variables in 34 Nebraska school districts. He found that one of the district variables contributing the most to variation in student achievement was the number of minorities reported in the district. He also found that increases in human resources as measured by teacher perceptions impacted variation in student achievement. The study utilized both school district data and an 80-item questionnaire that was administered to randomly selected teachers in each of the 34 districts. His study is limited, however, because of his small sample size and because of the special class of small school districts from which he gathered data.

Bryant, McLellan, & West, 2002

Commentary: The study identifies the author, the date, the purpose or nature of the study, the design, and the findings. Missing in this example is one important element—the research question(s). However, if you happen to be doing a dissertation that explores the relationship between school district characteristics and student achievement, this might be a study you would wish to know more about.

Example 3: Qualitative Dissertation Study

Wax, Wax, and Dumont (1989), for instance, spent a year with Sioux students on the Pine Ridge reservation in South Dakota. Their observations led them to argue that the key educational problems at Pine Ridge arose from a previously undocumented conflict (or "disharmony") between the indigenous culture of the students and the culture of the classroom. They noted that the teachers had no knowledge of Lakota, the native language of the students. Many of the younger students spoke little or no

(Continued)

(Continued)

English. It was observed that the pedagogical practices and the curriculum of the Pine Ridge schools were identical to those of mainstream American education and made no concessions to the inherited social and learning experiences of the Native American students.

Cantrell, 1992

Commentary: This example follows the conventional presentation of qualitative research. The review identifies the author, the type of method used, qualitative findings, and the transferability of the observed information to other populations.

One of the best ways to familiarize yourself with the conventional reporting of research is to read journal articles in your field. You will quickly gain a sense of the patterns that most scholars employ. The more complete you are in providing your readers with good information about other research, the more you build the foundation upon which your own work rests. I should also note that as you read and record the work of others, it is important that you be thorough in making sure you gather all needed information. Below I list the types of information you will want to save before you move on to another resource.

Information to Record

Author(s)
Title
Data
Publisher and place of publication
If journal, volume number and pages
Research purpose
Research question(s)
Method and scope of study
Findings of the study
Recommendations made by authors

Style Manuals and Formatting Conventions

"In 1928 editors and business managers of anthropological and psychological journals met to discuss the form of journal manuscripts and to write instructions for their preparation" (*Publication Manual of the APA*, 2001, p. xix). In so doing, these scholars initiated a force that has become a ritual for most doctoral students in education and the social sciences: the mastery of the intricacies of APA. APA is the familiar acronym for this style manual.

Dissertations are formal works of scholarship, and their authors are required to follow stylistic conventions. Every discipline has preferred if not required style manuals that govern the manner in which scholarly writing is presented in print form. These different stylistic conventions for writing vary a great deal. Therefore, it is wise to determine which convention is preferred in your discipline and by your advisor prior to beginning the work of reporting research. It is a far more economical use of your time to cite authors and prepare your list of references as you write, as contrasted with reformatting your entire proposal or dissertation to conform to a style manual after you have written a draft. You may wish to purchase software that will automatically organize your references according to different style manuals.

Brief descriptions of some of the most common style manuals (APA, Chicago, MLA, or CBE) can be found on the Web sites of many research libraries. When you know the style convention you will use, you should purchase the book or booklet that defines the style's rules. These become critical reference books for you.

> **Tip**
>
> If you use the APA style manual, remember that only articles cited in your text are to be included in the reference section at the end of your study. Know, also, that some supervisory committee members cross-check in-text citations and references for an exact correspondence.

You need also to be alert to the requirements of your institution relative to how the dissertation is presented in its final form. Here too there are expectations, governed mainly by the publishing requirements of *Dissertation Abstracts*. For example, the inside margin of your paper should be an inch and a quarter, while the top, right, and bottom margins should be an inch in width. Your study will become a book in the institution's library, so the quality of the paper is an issue in some universities. Some now permit digital submissions, and that practice is growing; still, conventions do apply.

One of the major reasons for the precision governing how you present the sources of your information and ideas has to do with your responsibility to other scholars. The source of your ideas or language, if it is not your own, should be easily traceable by another. In the APA style, this is called a parenthetical citation, that is, the placing of a reference citation in parentheses at the end of the phrase containing the quoted language or borrowed concept. Then, you place the full citation in the reference list at the end of your study. In other stylistic conventions, you achieve the same result with a numerical reference or with a footnote. Exactly how the citation is indicated in your text differs from style manual to style manual; how you list your references also differs depending on the style manual. The most commonly used style manuals in education and the social sciences are the following:

1. *Publication manual of the American Psychological Association* (Latest Edition). Washington, DC: APA.

2. Campbell, W. (Latest Edition). *Form and style in thesis writing.* Boston: Houghton-Mifflin.

3. *MLA handbook for writers of research papers, theses, and dissertations.* (Latest Edition). New York: Modern Language Association.

4. Turabian, K. (Latest Edition). *A manual for writers of term papers, theses, and dissertations.* Chicago: University of Chicago Press.

As I indicated earlier, the most popular style manual in educational fields is the one developed by the American Psychological Association. The APA style guide has been updated periodically and is now in its fifth edition. Although you can locate Web sites dealing with some of the content of APA, there is a great deal of very valuable advice in this publication and it is worth acquiring.

Common Mistakes in Conducting the Literature Review

There are some common mistakes made in conducting the literature review.

First, haste makes waste and produces inaccuracies. When a scholar carries out a hurried research review, he or she usually overlooks important material. Dissertation progress can be stopped in its tracks when the supervisory committee discovers that a critical body of relevant research has been undiscovered and not included. Check with your committee by e-mail. Ask if they have knowledge of significant research works that relate to your topic. Scour the conference program of the American Educational Association's annual meeting as well as other research association meetings for relevant research. Read widely and nationally. It is more than probable that a local or regional scholar will have published articles about your topic. Naturally, you will want to include this person's work in your literature review. For example, if you are researching some aspect of the school superintendence, it is likely a scholar in a local university may have written about this topic. There are, however, many national studies written about school superintendents, and some well-funded research projects have been carried out over the years. Think both locally and nationally.

Second, some dissertations rely far too heavily on secondary sources. Expressions of opinion, articles that rely on the work of others as the basis for their claims, or papers that argue for a particular set of values or beliefs do not constitute research reports. If the literature review is full of these types of sources, there is a reasonable chance that the supervisory committee may find it incomplete. A good example of a report that masquerades as research is the famous *A Nation at Risk* report from 1983. This is a very important document, but it is not a research report. Rather, this report is a compilation of selected research studies and of political and educational beliefs. Or, put slightly differently, the conclusions arrived at in the report are derived less from actual data and more from beliefs. Thus, while it is an important landmark, it should not be presented as if it were a research report.

Third, in writing up research reports, there is a tendency to concentrate on findings or conclusions of the study with little analysis of the method used to obtain those results. It is impossible for a reader to weigh the merit of a research study if there is no indication of how generalizable or adequate its findings might be. A quantitative study involving thousands of subjects will be more persuasive than a study involving ten. A qualitative study that involved the collection of "thick, rich" data from many sources via many contacts with research subjects will likely yield more persuasive conclusions than those from a study based on two interviews of 30 minutes each. All research is flawed. As a researcher, you need to be critical of every study you review.

Review of Discourse

For the nontraditional student, participation in the debates over research paradigms may be difficult. Suffice it to say that there are many. Much of what I have written about the literature review has been grounded in what some refer to as the positivist tradition. Even the label *literature review* is grounded in that tradition. If you are conducting a qualitative study and find the pattern I have described to be cumbersome and awkward, I recommend that you consider what Piantanida and Garman refer to as a *review of discourse* in contrast to a *review of literature*. These authors write:

> Too often, students seem to think in terms of a monolithic body of literature that is presented in one chapter of the proposal and subsequently transferred *in toto* to the dissertation. Reinforcing this view seems to be an assumption that the review of literature is a precursor to, rather than an integral part of, the study. (1999, p. 99)

When the concept of what constitutes literature is relieved of a narrow definition and broadened to include the entire spectrum of debate, writing, conversation, and policy discussion about a topic, you enter a community of discourse as opposed to a community of scholarship. In conducting qualitative research, this broadening of thought and opinion that you examine can be liberating.

Piantanida and Garman present a clear alternative to the approach to the literature review that I have provided. If you are interested in alternative approaches to constructing qualitative studies, I recommend that you familiarize yourself with the concepts explored by Piantanida and Garman (1999).

How to Use a Research Library

The most important tool you have in exploring the literature or discourse about your topic is the research library. In this discussion, I will help the nontraditional student understand the unique nature and resources of the research library. Furthermore, I will walk you through the steps and stages of using the resources of the research library. My discussion begins with the general characteristics of a research library. I then cover the significant changes that have taken place in how research libraries organize and provide access to their holdings. I next describe the types of databases that are now available to patrons and how you can access these services. I show how you can search a topic and provide an example of the results you might expect.

Supervisory committee members expect the student to gather research and use it in some part of the dissertation. It is assumed that, in doing this, the doctoral student will make use of the research library. The process of constructing a dissertation requires that the scholar systematically build a thorough knowledge of the research that has been done in the scholar's area of interest. The scholar does so by mining the resources of the research library. The knowledge of how to use a research library stands as one of the essential skills necessary to the completion of a doctoral dissertation. Many who work in libraries now refer to this skill as "information literacy" (Bundy, 1998). Implied by this term is the ability to understand and use the growing information resources of the research library. Most library resources now require technical skills and knowledge of databases as a precursor to searching for any information. For example, in educational research, a familiarity with the ERIC database is necessary. The researcher needs to be familiar with commercial products such as the Web of Science databases, *Dissertation Abstracts,* the Social Sciences Citation Index, and PSYCH Lit. Library staff now store literature in digitized databases in almost all disciplines.

Tip

Make sure that you have access to a major research library as part of your enrolled status as a doctoral student. Even if your institutional home does not have a research library, most doctoral programs have agreements with major libraries. Furthermore, most public universities with major research libraries have provisions for public use.

What Distinguishes a Research Library?

The nontraditional student may not live close to a research library, and not all doctoral programs are offered by institutions that support a major research library. It is important, therefore, for the nontraditional student to learn more about this essential and unique resource. How does the university research library differ from the local public library or the college library? There are many special characteristics of the research library. Here are some of them.

First, research libraries are usually located on the campus of a large research university. For years, such libraries pursued a mission of acquiring print materials and developing print collections and were known as places one could go to in order to gather information on a wide, wide array of topics. Recently, this has changed as research libraries have emphasized the new direction of providing information beyond their own particular collections and beyond the walls of their buildings. Research libraries do this by acquiring rights to various electronic databases, which they subscribe to but do not own.

National and international in scope, the research library does not focus its acquisition of materials on the local or regional. The research library is a tool for discovering in-depth material from the widest possible sources. For example, a person will not find the Catalogue of Early Christian Latin Texts in the local public library, but that person will probably find it in a large research library. A person will not usually find back editions of the local newspaper in the Research Library, but most public libraries do carry back editions of the local newspapers. It is customary for librarians in public libraries to maintain files of clippings about special topics. In fact, many libraries subscribe to services that do this compilation work for them. Research librarians do not maintain such files.

The research library is an instructional arm of a university. Its librarians are faculty members of the university. They are partners with other faculty colleagues in advancing knowledge. They develop ways for users to access collections; they develop search terms and databases so that researchers may access a wide array of sources. A major responsibility of library faculty members is to develop information literacy in the patrons or users of libraries.

The research library acquires or maintains collections of information in all kinds of disciplines and knowledge domains. An essential purpose of the research library is to support scholarly research. With links to other research libraries around the world, each university research library can be seen as a global repository of data and information. However, research libraries no longer serve only as a physical repository of huge amounts of print data. This is an important distinction. In recent years, as I indicated above, these institutions have begun providing access to information they do not own. Instead, the libraries provide their patrons with access to databases owned and maintained by others. The familiar ERIC database is an example. Research libraries do own their books and monographs. Even in this area, however, they purchase the software that allows a user to easily search the library's collection electronically. The old card catalog with its long narrow drawers full of bibliographic cards has been replaced with computer terminals. Furthermore, through

Internet connectivity, patrons can use their own computers to search a library's collection and databases without leaving their homes. This is a decided boon for the nontraditional student.

Library Developments in Perspective

The volume of information about various topics in education and the social sciences has grown exponentially. One of the responses of the research library has been to digitize its collections and serials in order to facilitate searches. This new development is of tremendous aid to all doctoral students and especially to the nontraditional student. These technical advances have facilitated the identification of relevant material and vastly improve access for the nontraditional student. One set of developments has to do with the ways that research librarians have redesigned access to the material they store. The second set of developments has to do with the way a patron searches for information once he or she has gained access.

Library Access

Beginning with the first set of transformations, access to research libraries has changed. For decades, a person had to physically walk through the doors of the research library. This door was the gateway to the information housed by the library. Often, the door was guarded and a person had to have some legitimate identification in order to enter. Librarians had neither the interest nor the capacity to make collections readily available to all users. Thus, for example, there were often priority lists defining who could access the collections in the stacks. Once inside the library, the scholar usually used the card catalog system to find the location of a book or journal she or he wanted to read. Then, armed with this information, the scholar either entered the stacks in search of the article or, in the case of closed stacks, gave the information about the book or article to a librarian who entered the stacks to retrieve the article. Some research libraries continue to restrict access to their stacks. But, access to holdings has changed. Research libraries have expanded access to all users.

Nowhere is this transformation more evident than in the area of electronic access. Users still need an ID in order to use the full resources of the research library. But, their ID can now be a password that allows them to enter the library through an electronic gate. This gate, a proxy server in most cases, symbolizes the changes that have taken place in terms of access. Now the gate is a virtual gate, and it opens not only to information housed in the library, but also to information housed in databases to which the library provides access.

Because of the new utilization of technology, a user or patron of the research library is able to access information from her or his computer terminal. As long as the user's computer is hooked to the Internet, that person may retrieve the same type and volume of information that he or she could get if sitting before a terminal within the library. This type of access is obviously a boon to the nontraditional student who typically finds it difficult to physically go to a library for long periods of time.

Creating this new system of access did not happen overnight. It went through several stages. Librarians began digitizing databases in the 1960s and 1970s. In the 1980s and early 1990s, storing vast amounts of material on CD-ROMs was common. As the power of the computer grew in terms of its storage capacity, librarians shifted their storage of databases to servers that could be accessed via networked systems. The most current stage is the Web-based system now used that permits full-text based searches.

Library Search Resources

1970s	1980s	1990s	2000
Physical Search	Terminal Use	Terminal/Windows	Terminal
Card Catalog	CD-ROM Search	Menu Driven	Multiple Search
Hand Search	Telnet, Command Language	Key word Search	Text Search

The table above charts the development in the digitizing of library holdings, the material formerly referenced in the card catalog. This process is referred to as "retrospective conversion of the central catalog" or "retrocon." Originally, a researcher searched the holdings using the card catalog. Next, a user could search those same holdings using a CD-ROM that contained all of the card catalog material. During the CD-ROM phase, it was common for libraries to have a cart with a computer and terminal on it. The computer was loaded with a CD-ROM with a particular database. The user searched using this terminal, this computer, and this CD-ROM. At night, the cart would be wheeled to a secure room. One of the obvious limitations to this system was that only one user at a time could access the database.

In the 1990s, networked systems were developed that permitted multiple users to search a given database stored on a library's server. This development also expanded the types of searches that could be conducted because more fields were added. For example, during this phase, searches by strings of text in the title became possible. Finally, the present Web-based system allows for off-site access and expanded search capacity. For example, many digitized databases are supporting full-text searches. In other words, now you can read the article from a journal on your monitor.

In addition to improving access, another transformation occurred during this time period. As information resources developed, it became clear that library resources would be unable to match the capacity of the technology. That is, the resources of most library staffs would be taxed past efficiency if all the digitizing and software creation were to be done in-house. Thus, the number of vendors offering software that could search library databases grew. These vendors provided both software and databases.

Innovative Interfaces, Inc., for example, became one of the vendors that research libraries used to develop a system for searching the library's holdings of books and monographs. This led to the development of software that could be leased to libraries. Libraries own their collections and take care of developing their collections, but external vendors provide the means of searching these collections. This situation has led to some fairly interesting labels as librarians named their electronic collections.

Nicknames for Digitized Library Collections

University of Nebraska–Lincoln = Iris
University of Colorado = Chinook
Harvard University = Hollis
Vanderbilt University = ACORN
University of Florida = webLUIS
Hofstra University = LEXICAT
University of Southern California = ARGO
Stanford University = Socrates
University of Oregon = Janus
University of Virginia = VIRGO
University of Toledo = UTMOST
Ohio State University = Oscar
Arizona State University = ASU Catalog
University of Texas–Austin = UTnetCat
University of South Carolina = USCAN

With these digitized catalog resources, much has changed. Once upon a time, a single library patron could look in a single file cabinet at a moment in time. It is now possible for multiple patrons to search a database at once. Once upon a time, a library patron could search the library's holdings only when the library was open for business. Now, the resources are there whenever one wishes to log in and access them. These changes benefit the nontraditional doctoral student.

Searching From a Distance

For many nontraditional doctoral students, traveling to the library is not always feasible. Therefore, it is important to establish the means of searching and acquiring material from off campus. Because the process for logging into a library from a distance will vary in the small details, the outline below is general. Research libraries have telephone help numbers for you to use, and often it is best to call and ask for assistance with your need. Below are some practical steps to take as you establish your ability to log in to the library from home or work.

Step 1: Evaluate the capacity of your home or work computer. If needed, contact the library help desk and ask if your software and computer will be able to make full use of new electronic databases.

Step 2: Obtain an identification number from your university that permits you to use the library.

Step 3: If you do not have it, establish Internet access with a local provider. Realize that sometimes employers have established what are called firewalls; these will deny you complete access to a library's server. Realize, also, that how you connect to the Internet has important implications for how fast you will be able to retrieve material. Phone modems are far slower than high-speed access alternatives.

Step 4: Using your Internet browser (Netscape, Explorer), link to the library's Web site.

Step 5: Search library information pages for a link to remote access.

Step 6: Read information about remote access.

Step 7: Learn about reconfiguring your browser.

Step 8: Follow the instructions for reconfiguring your browser. If necessary, call the library help number to reconfigure browser.

Step 9: When your home computer is fully connected to the library's browser, you are ready to begin searching databases.

Tip
Call your librarian for help. There is a staff person in most libraries assigned to help patrons from off campus learn how to connect to the library resources. You will save time and anxiety by phoning this person.

It is important to remember to reset your browser to the original settings when you are finished with your search. Realize this technology is constantly changing and that the need to adjust your computer may disappear as connectivity improves.

Defining Search Terms or Key Words

Now, what do you do? What is the most efficient way to begin to search for information about your topic? Most research librarians will tell you that before you actually search for literature about your topic, you should carefully construct a set of search terms. It can save you time if you contact a reference librarian and seek assistance in identifying key words and search terms. It is important to remember that research topics often have a history. The topic of today may have had a different set of identifying labels at a different point in time. For example, educational studies of truancy may now come under the label of "at-risk" children. The Platoon system once held features of block scheduling. Be alert to changes in nomenclature as you seek to define search terms. In educational fields, the ERIC database is the most comprehensive electronic source of information. This database can be a good place to start with a list of key words. Each citation provides key words identified by its author as germane to the content of the article. Looking through ERIC to see how others have labeled their work can be useful.

Example of Using Key Words to Search a Database

Often a person has a general idea of what she or he wants to study. Narrowing a general topic down to a doable dissertation is a process that involves successive iterations of the research questions and an understanding of what other scholars have studied. Below I offer an example of searching a database using key words.

ERIC has a well-constructed Web site that publicizes its wares and products. To access its Web site (realize this address or URL may have changed) go to www.ericfacility.net/extra/index.html.

Once you are logged on to this Web site, find *Search/browse ERIC Authority Files*. This link will take you to the Thesaurus. Click on the Thesaurus link and you will be able to browse the ERIC Thesaurus.

Let's say I am interested in leadership and want to know what leadership attributes are reputed to work best in school settings. If I browse the ERIC Thesaurus under the term *leadership*, I find the following:

Leader Participation

Leaderless Groups

Leaders

Leaders Guides

Leadership

Leadership Effectiveness

Leadership Qualities

Leadership Responsibility

Leadership Styles

Leadership Training

Now let's say that, of the above, I am interested in the qualities that leaders possess. If I browse the ERIC Thesaurus for search terms that relate to *leadership qualities*, I find the following:

Administrative Qualifications

Collegiality

Leaders

Leadership

Leadership Effectiveness

Leadership Qualities

Leadership Responsibility

Leadership Training

Prestige

Now let's say that the term *prestige* strikes me as particularly interesting. I begin to wonder if leaders possess some sort of prestige factor that attracts followers. I browse the ERIC Thesaurus using the term *prestige* and find the following:

Awards

Careers

Caste

Leadership Qualities

Popularity

Prestige

Professional Recognition

Reputation

Selective Colleges

Social Status

Status Need

In this way, you build a conceptual map around your main topic. Once you have found the particular aspect of your topic (leadership in the example above) on which you wish to concentrate, you will want to actually search the ERIC database for articles that use this descriptor to capture the nature of their research. A search using the key words *status* and *need* and *principal* yielded 84 citations, many of which seemed only tangentially connected to the concept of status need. A more targeted search using *status need* as a descriptor phrase and *principal* as a key word yielded only three citations, two of which were done by one scholar and were focused directly on the status need of administrators. Donald Willower studied pupil control ideology and explored the concept of status need in developing his theory about how administrators needed to control students. If this subject became your focus, a next step might be to search the Social Citations Index (available online through Web of Knowledge) to see who has cited Willower's work.

Thus, from a very broad interest in leadership, I have traveled to a very specific focus on the status needs of school leaders in terms of how pupil control beliefs satisfy that status need. Note, however, that nowhere did the search processes I used identify the study by Cuban that I used earlier as an example of an abstract. Yet, Cuban's study could teach me things about leadership as it was a case study of three role leaders. Any search will be incomplete. Your task is to make it as complete as you can.

Once you have key words or search terms, you should systematically begin to explore other resources. You will want to search the library's holdings, that is, their books and period-

> **Tip**
>
> Make sure you ask your advisor and your committee members to tell you of any studies or individual scholars that they believe you should include in your examination.

icals. You will want to look for journal articles in electronic databases. Below are instructions from the research library at the University of Nebraska—Lincoln (UNL).

How do I find books on a topic?

To find books on a specific topic, try a subject or keyword search on the UNL Libraries Catalog, which contains records for most of the printed books owned by the UNL Libraries.

How do I find journal articles on a topic?

It is important to choose a database or index that is appropriate to your research. Databases and indexes provided by the UNL Libraries can be found through Journal Indexes and Databases, which can be located under the Resources link on the IRIS Home Page.

Multi-subject resources such as Expanded Academic Index and Omnifile provide citations and full-text materials on a wide variety of topics. The databases include sources such as popular magazines, scholarly journals, and newspapers.

Subject-specific resources provide articles that relate to a specific discipline. Examples include ERIC, which provides sources in education, and PsycLit, which relates to the field of psychology and psychological aspects of related disciplines. These subject databases include resources in scholarly journals or books and chapters within books. Subject lists are also located under the Resources link on the IRIS Home Page.

How do I get books or journal articles that UNL Libraries do not own?

You can request materials that the UNL Libraries don't own through the Interlibrary Loan Department. The department provides online request forms that must be filled out in order to place a request.

Searching the Internet

The Internet is an obvious resource for finding information about a topic. If you recall the distinction I discussed earlier about a community of discourse (in referencing Piantanida and Garman), you will remember that a person can go beyond formal research. The Web is a source for information from the community of discourse. The Web is an ever-expanding repository of information. There are a number of common tools or search engines used to find information on the Internet. The utility of these search engines improves constantly. Learn from your research library about recommended search engines. Your library will have a list of these referenced on its home page and will include a description of how each search engine works.

One of the best online resources for assistance in searching the Web can be found at the University of South Carolina's Beaufort Library. BARE BONES 101 is an online tutorial on how to find information on the Web. You should read it.

It also is useful to know that some search engines have been designed to support searching through the use of truncation, the application of a wildcard character after a stem. Once a stem has been marked for truncation, the search will find any characters after the stem that are matched with your search term or key word. Usually an asterisk is used to designate the wildcard. Below is an example of how this works using a subject, *bird*, and the Alta Vista search engine.

Subject or Search Term	Document Counts
Bird	1,112,034
Birds	799,769
Birds*	1,834,510

These numbers or document counts will vary as more sites have been added since I performed this search. The asterisk instructs the *spider,* or file that is searching the database, to include any site that has characters after the stem, *bird.* Thus, sites with identifiers such as *birding, birdbrain,* or *birdie* are selected. Consequently, many more sites are identified with the conversion of the original term to a stem.

Evaluating Information From the Web

There are many issues associated with searches of the Internet. Web sites vary widely in terms of quality. The phrase *caveat emptor* certainly applies. Given the principle of providing unfettered access to information, few search engines limit what may be uploaded to the Web. It is up to the user to determine what is of value. Furthermore, the volume of information can be overwhelming. The comprehensiveness of different search engines varies. When you use a search engine to search the Web, you are not searching the entire Web. Rather, you are searching a portion of the Web captured at some point in the past by the architects of the particular search engine that you are using. Here are some of the suggestions made by research librarians relative to evaluating the quality of information found on the Internet.

- Web searches yield masses of information from memos to scholarly papers. Much of the information you get may be of little use.
- You should be able to identify the author of the material you wish to use.
- You should be able to have sufficient information about the author to make an informed judgment about that person's expertise.
- The location of the site should be identifiable.
- There should be an e-mail link so that you might ask questions or make comments.
- Don't take Web material as necessarily accurate. Web sites are rarely reviewed.
- Look for the source of any information in the material to see if you can determine whether the information is original or borrowed from elsewhere.
- Look to see if the site has been updated recently.
- Don't assume that links on the site are the most appropriate ones for what you are after.
- Test to see if links work as a measure of how well the site is maintained. (Jacobson & Cohen, 2003)

Summary

In this chapter, I have discussed the following conventions and behaviors:

1. The convention of the literature review

2. Types of research material

3. Academic rigor

4. Scope of the review

5. Organizing and presenting research literature

6. The use of the research library

7. Conventional search processes

8. The use of style manuals

9. Accessing the library

10. Using databases and search terms

11. Evaluating information

Up to this point, I have covered many important elements of the dissertation. One of the difficult tasks for the nontraditional student is collecting the research. A second difficult task is simply finding the time to do the searching and the reading required as a foundation for writing the dissertation. Paying attention to the sources of information and to the processes one can use in combing these sources for relevant scholarship should help you in crafting your study. If you have created a solid review of the research about your topic, you are well on your way to completing your proposal and to providing your study with a solid foundation.

4

The Research Design

Place all the above ingredients together in a large bowl and beat well. Dissolve two level teaspoons soda in one eighth cup of hot water. Add to beaten mixture. Sift in two cups flour. Beat well. Add one cup boiling water and beat lightly and quickly.

—Recipe for Evadne's
Gingerbread, in Rawlings, 1942, p. 168

In the traditional design of the dissertation proposal and dissertation, Chapter Three is reserved for a discussion and presentation of the method you will use to answer your research question. In this chapter you present the recipe you will use to make your "gingerbread." If you are doing a qualitative study, realize that you may not wish to utilize this convention of a separate chapter devoted to method.

What kind of data will you gather? From whom will you gather these data? If you will be gathering data from people, how will you choose the research subjects for your study? How will you ensure that you have adequate data to address your research question? How will you analyze your data? If your dissertation were a cake, this chapter would be the recipe both for making that cake and for judging how successfully the cake turned out.

A number of factors relate to your methodology. In this chapter of the book, I am not concerned with covering the many different quantitative and qualitative methods available to address research questions. There are many excellent methods books, and you should be in search of these texts. Rather, this chapter, based on experience in working with many doctoral students, covers important methodological issues students face in completing their dissertation studies: (1) the research design, (2) quantitative and qualitative issues, (3) getting good data, (4) objectivity and bias, and (5) the institutional review board (IRB). All appear as important decision areas for the nontraditional student.

In this chapter, you want to present a clear and detailed picture of what you are going to do. Your committee will want to feel confident that you can gather and analyze the information you need in order to answer your question. The task is to think through every step of your data gathering, the analysis of the data, and how you will report the results of your analysis.

Exploratory and Descriptive Studies

Atheoretical studies that intentionally set out to capture or describe a phenomenon are common. If you are exploring a topic in a very limited way, you may wish to call your study an exploratory study. This label might relieve you of a more rigorous standard that will be applied if you intend to gather data to establish or reject a belief or to question the value of a behavior or practice. In fact, many dissertations are exploratory studies. The objectives of such studies are tentative. Beware, however, you may have trouble making a case for an exploratory study of a topic thoroughly studied by other scholars, unless you intend to question the conclusions reached by those earlier explorers.

Another term commonly used to describe a dissertation's overall approach is to call it a *descriptive* study. This accomplishes a similar purpose. If what you are going to do is describe, you may relieve your study of an obligation to provide new meaning. That is, your intent is less to explain a phenomenon or a behavior than to describe it. Of course, such studies will be more interesting if what is being studied has never been described before. Developing a method to explore or describe is typically less of a challenge than developing a process for explaining the relationship between variables, testing a hypothesis, or proving a causal relationship. And, for the qualitative study, the in-depth examination of human experience requires a rigor and sustained involvement with subjects not normally found in exploratory or descriptive studies.

I should also note that some supervisory committees may reject descriptive or explanatory studies. Faculty committee members will want the study to attempt to add to the knowledge base about a topic. To do so requires interpretation and conclusions based on data no matter whether the research method is quantitative or qualitative.

One of the common discussions among students at the planning stages of the dissertation centers on this question: Shall I do a quantitative or a qualitative study? Below I discuss both generic types of methods.

Quantitative Studies

Over the past 50 years, large numbers of quantitative studies have sought to add to our knowledge of human society and how it works. Generally, doctoral dissertations utilizing various quantitative approaches identify a dependent variable(s) and seek to find out if one or more independent variables influence, impact, or change that dependent variable. By definition, an independent variable is one that varies independently of others. By definition, a dependent variable is presumed to be dependent on another variable or set of variables. For example, assume that we want to know what factors contribute to childhood obesity. Weight would be a dependent variable. All of the factors that we could identify and measure that we felt impacted weight would be listed as independent variables.

> **Tip**
>
> If you are planning a quantitative study, make sure to spell out very precisely and clearly the relationship between variables. Confusion about the relationship of variables is often a problem in the initial stages of creating a dissertation. You can save time and energy by developing these relationships early in your planning.

Typically, quantitative studies involve the gathering of data about or from human subjects, although the use of existing data is also common.

If you are conducting a quantitative study that involves the identification of research subjects, you should indicate every step you will take to identify those subjects. Who will these people be and how will you identify them? If you intend to sample a representative group, how will you conduct that sample? If, as part of such a study, you intend to see if you can prove or disprove a hypothesis about how

---

Tip

The Buros Institute publishes a very useful guide to mental measurements that is both an excellent source of instruments and an excellent source for reviews of instruments purporting to capture human attitudes and values. This resource is a virtual gold mine for doctoral students wanting validated instruments that measure human attitude.

---

these subjects behave, think, or feel, you will want to construct null hypotheses that you will test. If you are using a previously constructed instrument to measure the attitudes or beliefs of these subjects, you will want to carefully establish the veracity of that instrument.

In carrying out quantitative studies that use inferential statistics, you will want to consider the following issues:

1. Clear delineation of dependent and independent variables

2. Population, sample frame, and sample size issues

3. Questionnaire/instrument design

4. Number of cases

5. Type of data (nominal, ordinal, interval, ratio)

6. Statistical tests

7. Assumptions of the selected statistical test

8. Confidence levels

9. Null hypotheses

Tip

Students sometimes want to know if they can use the data from their pilot in their study. Usually a pilot is done as a preliminary to completing an IRB application. Since the purpose of the pilot is to fine tune and change the data-gathering process, you will not want to use data that might not be complete. And, because you are required to have formal consent from every subject prior to publishing any results from your data-gathering process, you should not use data from your pilot study in your full dissertation unless you have an IRB-approved informed consent letter signed by subjects.

Not all of these apply, depending on what you are doing. You may use all the subjects in a population as a data source. You may not be testing a hypothesis. But, no matter your particular quantitative research design, it is important to think through the whole process of subject selection, data gathering, data analysis, and reporting. All quantitative studies should be piloted before being fully implemented as there are almost always design quirks that a person doesn't discover until he or she sets out to gather and analyze data.

Careful planning in the steps of the qualitative study will enable the members of your supervisory committee to better help you at the proposal stage and feel more confidence in your findings at the conclusion of your study.

Qualitative Studies

If you are carrying out a qualitative study, a similar level of detail about method is appropriate, but the focus is different. In qualitative research studies, there are three big methodological challenges. The first is gathering enough data to address the research question; the second is dealing with the enormous quantity of qualitative data that results from a thorough investigation. A third challenge of a different sort occurs as you interpret the data and give meaning to what you have uncovered.

It is worth noting that, for many years, doctoral students in education and the social sciences felt, rightly or wrongly, that qualitative studies were somewhat suspect. This is no longer the case. Many dissertations employ various qualitative methodologies. Thus, there is no need for a lengthy defense or apology for the qualitative approach. There is, however, a clear need to indicate what qualitative method you will use and how you will improve your chances of locating the data and information you need to address your research question. What will be your sources of data, and what will you do with that information once you have it?

In gathering sufficient amounts of the right kind of data, many factors are important. Among them are these:

1. Identifying knowledgeable subjects

2. Gaining entry to the field

3. Earning trust of subjects

4. Achieving adequate exposure to the field

5. Asking probing questions

6. Strategizing how to build on existing data

7. Recording information

In terms of dealing with voluminous amounts of data, the following factors are important:

1. Organizing the data

2. Transcription

3. Veracity of data

4. Coding

5. Interpretation strategies

Organizing the Data

How will you deal with field notes, interview transcripts, historical documents, artifacts, and other text-based information that you gather? Somehow, in all of the text material, you have to find themes or recurrent ideas that you find of sufficient importance to help you answer your research question. There are various methods discussed in qualitative texts for organizing and searching voluminous amounts of text material. You will want to be clear about your intended approach for analyzing the qualitative data you collect. There are now software programs that you can purchase that will search text files for words or phrases that you identify. These can be valuable. Many qualitative scholars also recommend that you read your data. "Read, reread and once more read through the data," caution Rossman and Rallis (1998, p. 178). Have a plan in mind for dealing with your qualitative data before you gather it.

Transcription

Transcription is the hard work of the qualitative researcher who conducts interviews with subjects as a data-gathering strategy. It takes hours to transform the spoken words that you have taped into a written text. And this hard reality is one you must anticipate. For the nontraditional student with multiple obligations, transcription can be a very difficult task. Thus, be prepared to hire a person to do this work for you if necessary.

If your qualitative study involves interviews that must be coded, transcription is an element of your study that needs to be planned in advance.

> ### Tip
>
> If you transcribe data yourself, you would be wise to rent a transcription recorder that has been made for repeated stops and starts. A typical cassette recorder is driven by a rubber band that will stretch from repeated use. If you transcribe from such a machine, you will eventually wear out this band. Check to see if your university has a media center with such equipment. Public school districts might be another possible resource.

Veracity of the Data

Because the researcher is the screen through which most qualitative data flows, supervisory committee members often want to know what steps the doctoral researcher has in mind to ensure the truthfulness and accuracy of the data. Techniques for doing so include such approaches as member checking, audits of material and analysis, and triangulation. You will want to deal with this issue in your methods section.

Coding and Interpretation

Qualitative methods texts normally offer suggestions for how to code and interpret data. It is common to go through several iterations or stages in developing themes or recurrent ideas in qualitative data. It is also common to have a plan in mind for how you will interpret your qualitative data. You may wish to learn to use a software program to help you identify themes. Many have found these programs a significant aid.

It is also true that you may not do precisely what you plan to do relative to data analysis. Most supervisory committees understand that once the researcher is in the field, things may change.

Contingency Plans:
Changing the Research Design Plan

Things could be worse. Suppose your errors were counted and published every day, like those of a baseball player.

—Anonymous*

The dissertation proposal normally presents a plan for gathering data. The proposal may cover this plan in Chapter Three or in some other part of the proposal. The student's supervisory committee has approved a plan, and there is a common understanding as to what will be done. But, even when the plan is thoroughly circumscribed in advance, things may change for the researcher once the data-gathering process begins. What happens if the student discovers a need to alter the original plan? What degrees of freedom exist in terms of changing the research design?

Many supervisory committees will warn a student that there may be a need to modify an existing research design. In some instances, a student may be overly ambitious in terms of the number of subjects that will be used in a qualitative study. Knowing that the student will probably amass a mountain of data, the committee might advise the student to reduce the number of subjects. In a quantitative study, there may be a concern about the availability of research subjects. What will be done if some unforeseen circumstance compromises the design?

Here is an example. A student plans to do a study of teachers in a public school with a special focus. The school educates homeless children who live in a large urban area. There are six teachers in this school, and the doctoral student wants to explore the knowledge these teachers have of what works with this special population of homeless students. The committee meets. The study is approved. The doctoral student sets off for the first of a number of scheduled interviews with his subjects, interviews planned to take place over a seven-month period of time. After the first month of the study, two of the six teachers depart for other jobs. In the third month, another leaves. The school is in some disarray. Of the original six teachers, only three are left. What is the doctoral student to do? Can the student continue with his study?

Such happenings are common in doctoral research. Human beings are not like corn seedlings in an experimental plot under the control of the researcher. They change; things change. Supervisory committees understand this. For this reason, they often raise the necessary specter of the contingency plan. What will you do if your present design doesn't work? In the example above, the student continued with fewer subjects. This was acceptable to the committee, which felt that the student could still uncover sufficient data to address the research questions.

As part of your research design, it is wise to contemplate contingency plans. What will you do if your return rate on a survey is very low? What will you do if subjects drop out? What will you do if a factor analysis fails to clump variables together? What will you do if your plan to carry out a participant observation must be scuttled because things have changed at work and your boss tells you that you cannot have the released time upon which you counted? Many students experience problems in carrying out their research design. It is wise to develop contingency plans for those important requirements of your design that might prove to be a problem. Your supervisory committee can help you identify these problem areas and provide you with suggestions as to how you should proceed if you meet a major glitch.

Remember, the purpose of the research design is to present a plan that will result in good data.

Some Common Design Problems

Perfection in research is an oxymoron.

—Anonymous

I tell doctoral students that there is no such thing as the perfect research design. Every design has flaws. Some just have more serious flaws than others. Here is a short list of problems that I have found to be common in doctoral dissertations, problems that are not fatal (a negative vote of the supervisory committee) but that are best acknowledged in the methods chapter or in the reporting of the findings.

First, quantitative dissertation research is often done with small numbers. This means that there may simply not be enough cases in the study to result in statistical significance. For example, in a recently completed study of 34 school districts, researchers West (2002) and McLellan (2002) could find few school district variables that were statistically significant contributors to student achievement. However, had they included a thousand school districts in their study, they might have found more relationships between their dependent and independent variables. This problem is common; statistical texts label it the problem of *effect size.* You should understand this concept if you plan to report on the relationship of dependent and independent variables and if your design contains small numbers of units of analysis.

Another common issue involves the development of questionnaires. Is it valid to use an instrument that has not been validated? The answer is that it is not only permissible, it is common. The archives of dissertation research are full of questionnaires not validated by rigorous processes. But, many of these questionnaires gather descriptive information about what exists. Demographic data and respondent opinions about matters reported using a Likert scale require no elaborate validation process. The typical process of having a knowledgeable panel review a questionnaire along with a pilot study is usually sufficient in such studies. This is not the case when an instrument is created to do more than capture respondent demographics and respondent opinion.

Do the items on the questionnaire that make up the subscales truly belong in the subset to which you have allocated them? Specific concepts are sometimes established through factor analysis once the instrument has been used. Beware: If you do not have sufficient numbers of subjects in your study, you will not be able to carry out a factor analysis. When the design of the instrument includes scales or subscales that purport to measure human attitude or attributes, a more involved validation process is appropriate. Does the instrument really measure the concepts it claims to measure (such attributions as leadership, loyalty, internal locus of control, self-efficacy, motivation, and emotional intelligence)? If so, the most appropriate way to determine that the instrument really does capture variation in human attributes or attitudes is to subject it to a thorough test. Such a validation process will be more involved than many doctoral students can accept. To understand the validation process of such an instrument, refer to any modern text on measurement or read Thurston's classic 1928 article on this topic from the *American Journal of Sociology* titled "Attitudes Can Be Measured." Because this process is difficult, students often turn to a questionnaire that has already been validated and reviewed. The Buros Institute and its annual *Mental Measurement Yearbook* (Plake, Impara, & Spies, 2003) is an invaluable resource for those looking for instruments to measure human attitudes. This resource is now searchable electronically. Below is an example of the type of information that can be retrieved about instruments.

Descriptive Information

Title: Locus of Control of Behavior Scale
Author: Craig, A. R. Franklin, J. A. Andrews, Gavin
Abstract: The Locus of Control of Behavior Scale (LCB Scale) measures the propensity to relapse after behavior modification takes place. It consists of 17 items rated on a 6-point Likert-type scale. It is to be used with adults who are attempting a behavior change to predict which persons may need further help to inhibit the relapse before it occurs. Reliability and validity are discussed. (JW)

Test Acronyms: LCB Scale
Material Notes: 1. Article reprint. See availability source.
Publication Date: 1984
Most recent update to the database: Nov 1999
ETS Tracking Number: TC810806

Contact Information: For more detailed information about this measure and its related materials, please contact or consult: British Journal of Medical Psychology, 0007-1129, v57 p173-80, 1984.

Another common issue is that many studies are designed to gather information about perceptions, not actual facts. This usually poses no problem as long as the researcher does not report findings as if they were fact. In reporting the results of such a survey of perceptions, a researcher must remember that it is opinions, not facts, which have been gathered. Thus, the researcher reports the results as perceptions. The title should indicate that perceptions are reported, as should the abstract of the study. If you examine *Dissertation Abstracts* carefully, you will locate more than a few dissertations that present subject perceptions as facts. If you want to establish causal or factual relations, you need to build an instrument that will measure such relationships.

Fenwick English, in an article that challenged prevalent practice in educational research, noted how common is the research design that can't help but be successful in yielding a positive relationship between dependent and independent variables because both measure the same thing (English, 2002). That is, if I *operationalize* a dependent and independent variable with similar measures, I increase the probability of a strong positive correlation. English rightly cautions against a design that begins with this unanalyzed colinearity between dependent and independent variables. If you do a study using measures that might be capturing the same phenomenon, make sure that you examine colinearity between variables.

Another related issue is that sometimes the research question or the definition of the variables in the study leads to a grand tautology. What does this mean? A tautology is a statement so broad and inclusive as to embrace everything: How do one's life experiences influence one's leadership style? Such a question is far too nonspecific and will lead to circular reasoning. By definition, everything in a person's experience shapes that person's behavior. Of course it is true that somewhere in a person's experiences will be something that shapes how that person behaves in a leadership position. The question provides no guide to help identify any particular set of factors that might be more important than others. Avoid these types of questions.

Getting Good Data

You can't expect to hit the jackpot if you don't put a few nickels in the machine.

—Unknown

In order to complete your study convincingly and end up with something to say, you need good data. This requires planning. If you have not been well versed in research methods through coursework, the data-gathering portion of your study may give you problems. Be alert to the wealth of written resources about different research methods. There are many books about writing dissertations, about designing research studies, and about quantitative and qualitative methods. Students can use computer software to perform statistical analyses on data, to organize references and citations, and to carry out the detailed and voluminous work of quantitative data analysis.

Once you have determined your research question and the research method that you will use to gather data, begin to build your library about that method and research topic. You will want to read about your topic as you construct the literature review and about your method as you plan how you will gather and analyze data.

> ### Tip
>
> The use of Web-based surveys is becoming more common, and this technology can be a very useful way of carrying out a survey. But, it is also common for such designs to have serious glitches. If you intend to gather data using a Web-based survey, make sure you pilot the process carefully before committing to it.

The whole purpose of having a separate section of your dissertation or proposal devoted exclusively to methodology has to do with the single aim of getting good data and answering your research question in a convincing manner. If your study is a quantitative study, good data means data that exist in (1) appropriate type, (2) sufficient quantity, and (3) a satisfactory distribution that permits the type of analysis you intend to perform. If you wish to use statistical tests that rely on measures of central tendency, for example, you will expect your data to distribute normally. A bimodal distribution would violate the assumptions of many statistical tests. You also want data that you can trust. If you use a survey, you will want to know that the survey measures what you intend to measure.

If your method is qualitative, the same basic goal remains. You want data rich in detail that will give an adequate base for analysis. One interview of one subject for one hour is very unlikely to give you much with which to work. On the other hand, 10 interviews of that same subject over a period of time may give you more data than you can manage. Participant observation, done well, also provides a researcher with very useful qualitative data. Qualitative studies that utilize multiple data sources typically prove more persuasive than studies that do not.

Gathering data from people or contexts with whom or with which the qualitative researcher is quite familiar can pose a problem as well. Generally, it is wise for the researcher not to conduct qualitative research within his or her work environment or with people well known to the researcher. There are many reasons for this but paramount among these is the probability that the researcher either will not get good data or will not be able to fully utilize the data collected. In terms of having difficulty getting good data, it is hard for the qualitative researcher to see the forest for the trees when working in a familiar setting. Because we know the environment, we will make assumptions about what others know—a behavior we are far less likely to display when exploring an unfamiliar research setting. We allow our assumptions to stand in place of the qualitative data we might normally collect.

Objectivity and Bias

Get it right or let it alone. The conclusions you jump to may be your own.

—James Thurber, 1956

Another reason why this chapter on methodology is important is that it provides you with an opportunity to think about objectivity and bias. Doctoral research is set against a standard of objectivity. When you report your findings, those findings should be based on the data that you have collected. If your opinion takes precedence over what your data suggest, you are relaxing the standard of objectivity in favor of your subjective opinions. There is a place for this subjectivity but it is not in the ignoring of your data. This is a particularly important caveat for qualitative research.

Because the qualitative researcher is almost always the filter through which all data are processed, how does a researcher guard against finding only those answers that he or she wishes to find? That is the question James Thurber raises in his quote above. The issue is guarding against bias. Bias has the opportunity to occur at many points in a qualitative study. The researcher's subjective filter is in operation from the moment the study is chosen to the final recommendations made at the conclusion of the study. Some have argued that this very subjectivity is inescapable, that even the most objective of quantitative studies will be dependent upon a subjective epistemology. However, the philosophical debate over how we know reality is not the issue here. When doctoral students conduct a dissertation study, they are urged, if not required, to make some claims about the way the world works. Doctoral students need to make claims or conclusions based on evidence and logical reasoning.

Merriam (1998) wrote that in qualitative research, "the researcher is the primary instrument for data collection and analysis" (p. 7). Subjective bias in these two areas can lead the researcher inexorably down a path where claims will be made that cannot be supported. In the matter of data collection, some doctoral dissertations fall short. This is usually because the researcher does not have an adequate design for gathering data.

Here is an example. A researcher who is a female high school principal wants to study other female principals who have been recognized as excellent leaders and educators. You can quickly sense the common circumstance in which the doctoral student chooses to study a topic of personal importance. This researcher's choice of a subject is both a liability and a strength. She will be well versed in the issues, conflicts, and rewards associated with being a woman in a leadership position often (until recently) reserved for men. But, she will also bring her own experiences to her study and will filter what she learns and sees through those experiences. Thus, she may end up seeing more of herself in her subjects than is warranted. This would be a bias. If it were an influence, such a bias would tend to lead her toward miraculous conclusions about the experiences of women high school principals. These would be miraculous because, as is characteristic of miracles, conclusions would be drawn based more on faith than on evidence. Richard Nunnely, of the University of Minnesota—Twin Cities, has noted the mysterious ways that doctoral students will draw conclusions from very limited qualitative data. He remarked that he has often seen "great miracles happen at the end of the dissertation" (Nunnely, personal communication, September 12, 2000). Avoid miracles.

None of us is free from bias. Our predilections show up in how we ask questions, in what we leave out of our studies, and in how we interpret our results. There is an

---

Tip

The exhortation to be wary of bias does not mean the researcher eschews the first person voice in writing. There are many times when the first person is the right voice and when the student is right to acknowledge and honor his or her role as the lens through which the field is seen. Wolcott (1990) provides a view on this perspective full of common sense and free of research dogma.

obligation we assume to try to find ways to guard against these biases. In your chapter on method, you will want to address the issue of bias.

The Institutional Review Board

Men are men, then needs must err.

—Euripides*

For many years, institutions that receive federal funds of any kind have been required to demonstrate that all due care is taken to protect any human beings who are part of their research. As the quote from Euripides suggests, it is in our nature to make errors. Thus, any research that intends to gather data about or from human subjects must be reviewed by an institutional committee set up to protect human beings from harm. On many campuses, this committee is designated as the institutional review board. Before a doctoral candidate can gather data about or from human beings, the student must secure approval from this review board. If this is not done, the institution is under the substantial risk of losing federal funding. Because of

> **Tip**
>
> Realize that you are required to have permission to gather data before you gather data. This permission must be in writing and you must have a designated number for your research project and an approved consent process as part of your study.

this threat, universities take this obligation to follow federal guidelines for conducting research with great seriousness.

This review committee will, if your dissertation deals with human subjects, provide oversight to your study. It will want you to follow a standard process for informing subjects of their rights and of the guarantee that no harm will come to them if they participate in your project. Or, if participation does entail some risk, the process of gaining approval from the institutional review board to carry out the research must indicate that risk and subjects must be informed.

Proposed studies fall into three basic categories of review: (1) exempt review, (2) expedited review, and (3) full-board review. The first means that your subjects might be consenting adults, that you will be gathering data that cannot be identified with a particular person, that your subjects are public employees, or the like. An exempt review means that your purposes and design are so obvious that your study need not be subjected to much oversight. An expedited review is one in which a proposal is reviewed by a subcommittee or administrator of the institutional review board to assess the potential risk to study subjects. If your subjects are under the age of 19, or if there is the potential risk that one of your subjects might suffer some harm if identified, your study may be targeted for an expedited review. Finally, if there is serious risk, your study will be sent to the full institutional review board. A research proposal, for example, that intended to apply an intervention to preadolescent children with poor self-image would be the type of study that would face a full-board review. A classroom study of middle school students and their family lives would be another example. In both, there is potential risk to subjects. In the first, the intervention might hurt children. In the second, the researcher might uncover information of an illegal or harmful nature that would require reporting to authorities.

All universities that receive federal dollars have forms and a process for obtaining approval. The forms that you must complete are usually available online and you may download them. Your institutional review board provides phone numbers so that you can ask for assistance.

The review board will usually be composed of faculty members who have volunteered to serve. An administrative unit will provide support and structure and will work to ensure compliance on the part of members of the university community. These people take their work seriously because violations of federal law can result in very serious penalties.

Below is a guide to the classification terminology used by review boards.

Determining Level of Review		
Risk	*Participants Nonvulnerable*	*Participants Vulnerable*
Less than minimal	Exempt	Expedited or full board
Minimal	Expedited	Full board
Greater than minimal	Full board	Full board

The usual format of the application requires answers to the following:

1. Describe the project and its purpose (briefly).

2. Describe the research methods and procedures.

3. Describe the participants.

4. Describe benefits and risks to participants.

5. Describe recruiting procedures.

6. Justify the exempt status of the research.

7. Provide a copy of the informed consent (shown on next page).

8. State how informed consent will be obtained.

9. Provide a copy of a questionnaire, survey, or testing instrument.

10. Provide copies of institutional or organizational approvals.

11. Provide a copy of the funding proposal if appropriate.

Review boards are usually responsive to questions you may have. It is a good idea to work on your application or request for a review as you construct your dissertation proposal. In so doing, you will become more mindful of the types of issues that you will face in seeking permission to do your study. In fact, some institutions require an IRB approval as a condition of the proposal approval.

If your study will require an expedited or full-board review, realize that this will take time and plan accordingly. Such a review involves a meeting of a committee of faculty members to scrutinize your research proposal. You will probably have to do most of the work in securing approval. A phone call or e-mail to the person who manages the application process will facilitate this application. No matter the level of review, make sure you find out what is required for you to do in order to have your study approved. Approval needs to occur before you begin to gather data. There are a few horror stories of studies that have suffered because such approval was not obtained.

Most campuses now have a Web site on which you can locate necessary forms and information about completing this part of your study. You will need to accept responsibility for completing an application and securing approval. This can be done prior to a meeting to approve your proposal, although usually it is better to wait until you know your supervisory committee is content with what you plan to

Letterhead On Official Letterhead of Your Institution
IRB# 001001001

Informed Consent Information

Title

Project Title: Campus Climate and Needs Assessment Study for Gay, Lesbian, Bisexual, and Transgender Students

Purpose

Purpose of the Study: I am conducting a study of the UNL campus climate as it pertains to Gay, Lesbian, Bisexual, and Transgender (GLBT) students for the purpose of improving the learning environment of all students on campus. You are being invited to participate in this study. As a faculty, administrator, or staff member, your honest and candid perceptions regarding GLBT issues will help us understand how campus experiences impact everyone on campus. The results of this study will be useful in improving the campus for all.

Procedures

Methods and Procedures: We are asking you to complete a short survey indicating your experiences on campus as they relate to GLBT students and your attitudes regarding GLBT issues.

Time

Time to Participate: This will take about 10-15 minutes. When completed, please fold it over, staple or scotch tape it, and return it in campus mail to the address on the back.

Risks

Risks and/or Discomforts: There are no known risks or discomforts associated with this research.

Benefits

Benefits: Information gathered from this study will be used to improve the campus learning environment for GLBT students and in turn for all students.

(Continued)

(Continued)

Confidentiality   Confidentiality: The surveys completed for this study will not identify you by name. The surveys are anonymous and in no way will we be able to determine who answered what to any specific question. As soon as your survey is returned, your responses will be coded onto an answer sheet, your survey sheet will be destroyed, and only group responses will be reported. Records for this study will be kept in a locked cabinet in the university investigator's office and will only be seen by the investigators. Records will be stored for no longer than two years after the study is complete. Results will be reported so that no specific individual or department will be identified by name.

Compensation   Compensation: You will not receive any monetary compensation for participating in this project.

Opportunity to Ask Questions   Opportunity to Ask Questions: You may ask questions concerning this research and have those questions answered before agreeing to participate. Or, you may call Dr. _____ (phone number) to discuss your questions or concerns. If you have any questions about your rights as a participant in this study that have not been answered by the investigator, you may contact the Institutional Review Board (phone number).

Freedom to Withdraw   Freedom to Withdraw: You are free to decide not to participate in this study or to withdraw at any time without adversely affecting your relationship with the investigators or with the institution. Your decision will not result in any loss of benefits to which you are otherwise entitled.

Consent   Consent: Your completion of the attached survey will signify your consent to participate in this study after having read and understood the information presented above. Keep this copy of the consent information for your records.

> **Tip**
>
> Make sure you check with your advisor about whether you must complete a training program in human subjects research as a precondition of applying for IRB approval.

do. The best plan is to have a draft of a review board proposal ready at the time you present your study to your committee. Some institutions now require that you submit an IRB application at the same time as you submit your proposal. And, importantly, an increasing number of institutions require training in research standards for human subjects as a condition of IRB approval. You may have to participate in such training.

Because a strict adherence to convention has become the norm in recent years, I show an example of an informed consent letter that conforms to the IRB expectations for an exempt study. Be attentive to the details in this letter.

The main reason for my emphasis on this institutional review board process is that the federal government will probably establish a required IRB certification process for universities that receive federal funding. Universities that fail to comply with federal expectations will not be certified. This would be an outcome with devastating consequences for research institutions.

Summary

In discussing the chapter on research method, I have provided some general language for the different types of studies common to doctoral work, discussed the need for contingency planning, and indicated the importance of striving for objectivity and of developing a design that will help you get good data. Finally, this chapter has covered a very important part of the dissertation process dealing with your university's institutional review board.

5

The Report of
Your Findings

I f the matter of style has not yet become an issue for you, it may in the next two chapters. A little classic book by Strunk and White contains a true statement about writing style:

> Style is an increment in writing. When we speak of Fitzgerald's style, we don't mean his command of the relative pronoun, we mean the sound his words make on paper. Every writer, by the way he uses the language, reveals something of his spirit, his habits, his capacities, his bias. This is inevitable, as well as enjoyable. All writing is communication.*

Strunk and White (2000) offer us these suggestions about writing:

1. Place yourself in the background.

2. Write in a way that comes naturally.

3. Work from a suitable design.

---

*Excerpt pp. 66–67 from *The Elements of Style*, 4th ed., by William Strunk, Jr. and E. B. White. Copyright © 2000 by Allyn & Bacon. Reprinted by permission of Pearson Education, Inc.

4. Write with nouns and verbs.

5. Revise and rewrite.

6. Do not overwrite.

7. Do not overstate.

8. Avoid the use of qualifiers.

9. Do not affect a breezy manner.

10. Use orthodox spelling.

11. Do not explain too much.

12. Do not construct awkward adverbs.

13. Make sure the reader knows who is speaking.

14. Avoid fancy words.

15. Be clear.

The writing in your introductory chapter and in your literature review may be shaped by convention. The literature review tends to be stylized; the method you describe is shaped by a certain degree of dogma. In these latter chapters, you have the freedom to speak force-fully through the written word. Thus, your style can become an important rhetorical tool. Read what Strunk and White say about style. Their thoughts may be inspiring for you.

This does not mean there are not conventional expectations regarding the final chapters of dissertations. There are. But it is in these chapters that you can shape the reception of your ideas through the force of your rhetoric.

Conventions Guiding the Reporting of Data

You never know what is enough unless you know what is more than enough.

—William Blake[4]

You have your data! The collecting phase is completed. Now what? What did you find out? Convention reserves a chapter of your dissertation for the reporting of your data. Usually this is Chapter Four, although in some qualitative studies, the fourth chapter is not limited to the reporting of findings and includes a discussion of those findings. How do you meet this challenge, and what is expected in the conventional Chapter Four or in the reporting of data?

Conventions in the Reporting of Data

A Reminder of the Research Focus
An Objective Presentation of the Data
An Explication of the Research Process Used to
Analyze Data
The Reduction of Data
Interactions With Advisor
Organization of Findings
Reporting Data in Charts and Graphs
First-Person Voice
Writing to Discover in Chapters Four and Five
Redundancy
Ending With a Summary

Reminder of the Research Focus

It does no harm to remind the reader of the focus of the study and what you intended to accomplish. However, keep this section brief if you begin this chapter with such a reminder.

Objective Presentation

There is no particular order that dictates how you organize this chapter, although many writers allow their research questions to shape the chapter. It is helpful at this point to reiterate three standards that shape the expectations of the research community of which you are a part:

1. The standard of objectivity

2. The standard of clarity

3. The standard of replicability

First, a dissertation study sets out to address a question or issue by gathering evidence. Your committee will expect that you will present your data or information in such a way that others interested in the same topic will be able to use what you share in their own research. This is the standard of objectivity that is expected.

Second, the committee members (as well as other scholars) will expect that they can examine your data to see if they would reach the same conclusions as you reach. The dissertation is by definition a supervised piece of research. Your committee will want to be able to track how you interpreted your data. Any conclusion or recommendation reported in your study should be clearly related to evidence reported in this chapter. This is the standard of clarity. A reader should have no trouble understanding the data you have gathered. This is a second challenge for Chapter Four.

Third, dissertation research is normally held to a standard of replicability. That is, future scholars should find enough detail in your method and in the data you present that they could pattern their studies after yours. This standard of replicability is rarely fully achieved because most studies in social science fields involving human subjects cannot be replicated. Nonetheless, the standard of replicability remains as a goal. These three standards or expectations of scholarly research form the basis for the conventional reporting of data in Chapter Four.

Explication of Research Process

Chapter Four of the dissertation contains the reporting of the results of your study—it is the place where you present your findings. Information about your subjects, descriptive statistics, demographics, tables, lists of major themes, the results of statistical analysis, the results of axial coding, full descriptions of cases—these and other types of findings are reported in Chapter Four. If you used a *small n design*, this would be where you would present baseline data and intervention data for each of your subjects.

It is useful to provide an outline of the contents of this chapter at the beginning. Often a reader will have difficulty tracking the reporting of the data, particularly if there are many relationships being addressed or if qualitative data are voluminous. Thus, once you know how you will be presenting your data, give the reader a summary outline of this presentation at the beginning of the chapter. Avoid, however, the redundancy of repeating everything you wrote in your method chapter.

Data Reduction

Chapter Four is all about presenting data and reducing data. In this section, you should present sufficient data to answer your research question(s) and to support any conclusions you make. At the same time, most researchers must make sense of their data, and this typically requires some form of data reduction. If your study is quantitative, you may not wish to provide all of the data you analyzed. You will certainly wish to provide descriptive statistics and report the results of the various statistical tests that you ran.

You do not need to place histograms and frequency tables of every variable in your study in this chapter. Do descriptive statistics on all variables, but save much of

> ### Tip
>
> It is a common practice of careful quantitative researchers to examine their data carefully for abnormalities. Perhaps a number in a column was mistyped. Perhaps a response is miscoded. The data set without glitches is rare. So, eyeball your data. Look carefully not only at your descriptive statistics but directly at the numbers in their rows and columns.

this information for an appendix. Present the summaries of your data and the results of statistical tests. In presenting data in tables, examine the APA style guide carefully for the correct presentation formats. As you may guess, conventions abound in the manner of presenting quantitative data. Your particular statistical analysis will have a proscribed manner of presentation.

If your study is qualitative, you will want to provide a complete picture of the constant comparative analysis you did or of the coding you pursued to arrive at a set of themes or conclusions about your subject. Again, you need not provide detailed transcriptions of interviews or lengthy field notes here. Save these for an appendix.

In both instances, you are reducing data complexity. Wolcott has a very useful discussion of how to deal with voluminous amounts of material in a qualitative study (1990, pp. 63–70). He also offers this good advice: "Display formats provide alternatives for coping with two of our most critical tasks, data reduction and data analysis" (1990, p. 63). And, he noted about qualitative data, "the critical task in qualitative research is not to accumulate all the data you can, but to *can* (i.e., get rid of) most of the data you accumulate" (1990, p. 35).

Many students make use of appendices as a means of reporting the full information they collected, and this is a good strategy. Often, supervisory committee members will want to look at the raw data with which you worked. And, if the full data are presented, future researchers will also have access to it.

Interactions With Your Advisor During This Phase

It is also a convention that you communicate with your advisor as you attribute meaning to your data. Don't neglect to do this. Students often worry as to how they should present the material in Chapter Four to their advisor. Do they wait and give the advisor the finished product, including a final chapter, or do they feed drafts of each version of this chapter reporting the findings to their advisor? Do they provide all the members of the supervisory committee with draft copies? Similar questions arise with the concluding chapter of the dissertation. In almost all instances, you should contact your advisor to learn how she or he would like you to proceed. Different faculty advisors have distinctly different notions as to how they wish to monitor the pieces of a dissertation study, including the presentation of data.

To some degree, the presentation of data in quantitative studies will probably follow the research questions. Typically in quantitative studies, one begins with descriptive statistics and then moves on to present the results of statistical tests. One has several options in terms of discussing the meaning of the data. One may offer interpretations as one presents the data and the statistical results, or one may simply present the data and save the analysis for the subsequent chapter.

In terms of constructing meaning from your qualitative data, different qualitative research approaches suggest different procedures such as constant comparison or axial coding. The critical point is that you, the researcher, must construct meaning where no meaning is necessarily obvious. This is what the writers about qualitative research mean when they note that the researcher is the subjective lens through which the data are known. But, as I note shortly, interpreting qualitative data

> **Tip**
>
> It is a matter so obvious as to deserve little comment, but the annals of dissertation writing are full of horror stories of lost data and text. Back up your work constantly. Get a Zip drive that will accommodate a large amount of data and use this drive compulsively.

can be the fun part of the dissertation. Here are a few suggestions to help you in this regard.

1. Spend a great deal of time with your data.

2. Read what others have written about your subjects.

3. Read a few excellent examples of qualitative research.

4. Create alternative explanations of your data.

5. Have someone from another culture discuss your data.

6. Be playful; try out your interpretations on others.

7. E-mail your advisor with your ideas.

8. Bounce your interpretations off your subjects.

The clear attempt is to expand the number of eyes that look at your data and to expand your understandings. Constructing meaning is almost always a richer process when it accommodates multiple understandings.

Organization of Findings

There are standard ways to organize this chapter. You may elect to organize your findings according to your research questions; this is a common pattern. You may elect to organize this section chronologically in terms of how you conducted your analysis. You may wish to order it according to your significant findings, or you may wish to follow your own individualistic pattern.

No matter how you organize the chapter, recognize the value of summaries and of graphic representation. Dissertations often address many questions and appear complex to the reader. Thus, summaries of findings are very useful ways to convey complex information to your committee members and others. In addition, many studies explore relationships between ideas or theories and human behavior. If it is at all possible, find a way of displaying those relationships in graphic form. Such a presentation will aid you in depicting what you found and will aid your reader in understanding your study.

If your study is an elaborate one with many research questions and subquestions, this chapter will be elaborate as well. If your study is one using a multifactor analysis with a number of dependent and independent variables, this chapter will include a number of tables reporting the relationships of these variables. Commonly accepted conventions regarding spelling, punctuation, capitalization, and abbreviations as well as useful reminders about grammatical constructions appear in well-organized sections of the APA manual. One of the issues the researcher usually faces by the time she or he constructs the fourth chapter, if not before, is the matter of headings. Below is what APA requires in terms of format.

CENTERED UPPERCASE HEADING (Level 5)

Centered Uppercase and Lowercase Heading (Level 1)

Centered, Italicized, Uppercase and Lowercase Heading (Level 2)

Flush Left, Italicized, Uppercase and Lowercase Side Heading (Level 3)

Indented, italicized, lowercase and uppercase heading ending with a period. (Level 4)

In approaching the writing up of your data, you might benefit from looking at a book by Rudestam and Newton called *Surviving Your Dissertation* (1992). The section in this book called "Presenting the Results of Empirical Studies" is full of helpful ideas.

Make sure you familiarize yourself with how both your style manual (APA, MLA, or other) and your graduate college expect you to present data in tables and figures. Note also that unlike many professional journals, the guidelines for dissertations require you to place tables and figures in the text. Do not substitute "Table X about here" for the actual table. Put it in the text. This requirement may result in formatting issues for your word processor. If so, delay inserting the table or figure until later drafts. Eventually you will have to spend the time and energy to format tables, graphs, and figures so that they can be incorporated into the text of your dissertation.

Reporting Data in Tables, Charts, and Graphs

It is important to remember this about all tables, charts, graphs, and figures: You should (1) introduce the table, graphic, or figure;

(2) present the table, graphic, or figure; and (3) then discuss the table, graphic, or figure. Do not just insert a table, graphic, or figure with no introduction or commentary. Remember, also, that when your dissertation is bound, you need an inch-and-a-half margin on the left. Guard against intruding into that margin with a table, graphic, or figure.

First-Person Voice

Should we be worried that a smoke alarm will blare in our ears when the ethnography grows perilously hot and "too personal"?

—Behar, 1996, p. 7

It is appropriate to note that in Chapter Four of the qualitative study, a scholar may elect to write about her or his role as an integral part of the study. In such instances, the nontraditional student may face this question: Is it all right to write in the first person, using "I"? The use of the first-person voice is an issue that still surfaces with some faculty members. Some supervisory committee members adopt the philosophical stance of the positivist scholar holding that writing in the first person violates standards of objectivity. But, there is plenty of precedent to justify the use of the first person in dissertations. While you will find that most studies are written in the third person, many qualitative studies would be awkward if there were no room for personal expressions. There are clearly times when it is appropriate for a qualitative researcher to use the first person. One of the most compelling discussions I have read about the place of the scholar as a first-person persona in the study is by Ruth Behar. Behar (1996) writes about *writing vulnerably* as an anthropologist. In one sense she speaks of the emotional connection the qualitative researcher has to her or his subjects. If you have a wish to place yourself in your study, to honor your own presence in what you explore, to have your work be personal, Behar's *The Vulnerable Observer* is a book you should read. If you are attracted by the scholarship Behar describes, you will need to question many of the conventions discussed in this book.

Check with your advisor on this matter of straying from the conventions of third-person and objective voice.

Writing to Discover in Chapters Four and Five

The researcher begins with interesting, curious, or anomalous phenomena, which he observes, discovers, or stumbles across.

—Marshall and Rossman, 1989

At this point in the dissertation process, the nontraditional student is out there on his or her own. Hopefully you have a peer group with whom you can share your ideas. But even with such a support, you still have to do the interpretive work of making meaning. You are immersed in the reality of solo scholarship.

The act of sitting down and writing about your data can be unnerving to some researchers. Faced with this task, some doctoral students experience a form of writer's paralysis and just cannot get going. One of the solutions to this paralysis is not particularly economical in the short run but may be quite economical in the long run. That solution is to write to discover. This means that you start writing even if you do not have a clear scheme in mind and even if you do not have a clear picture of what your data reveal. This approach results in false starts and written material that you will probably discard. But, it is a way around the paralysis that sometimes occurs. Hence, in the long run, such an approach may be a key element in successfully completing the study.

Many a doctoral advisor has told a student to begin by just writing. In the first part of his book, *Writing Up Qualitative Research*, Wolcott (1990) captures many of the approaches taken by scholars to begin and sustain writing. If you are apprehensive about sitting down to begin writing, you will find his comments friendly and enormously helpful. Of course, it is one thing to just say, *"Start writing!"* It is quite another to actually do it. There are several strategies you can use to help stimulate action on your part:

1. Pretend you are at a meeting of practitioners in your field and tell them what you think is valuable about your study; do this out loud and tape yourself.

2. Write about what it might mean if your data are right.

3. Write about what it might mean if your data are wrong.

4. Write about what your data do not tell you about your research question.

In doing exercises of these sorts, it makes sense not to worry about grammar, spelling, and format.

The purpose of the exercise is not to write the final chapters; rather, the purpose is to move beyond your writer's block and generate ideas from your data that you will use in the formal writing of your final sections. As you "write to discover," you should soon begin to feel more comfortable with your understandings about your data, about what is meaningful, and about how you wish to structure this chapter.

In the exercise of writing to discover, form in writing is not as important as content. Eventually you will need to edit what you have written for errors.

> **Tip**
>
> Some people think more creatively when speaking than when writing. If you have this proclivity, form a conversation group and talk out loud about your data. Use your dissertation support group if you have one. If not, find some peers that will listen. Tape your conversation. You may glean important ideas as you listen to what you said when your thoughts were flowing freely. Ultimately the dissertation is a written document, so eventually you will have to convert your ideas to the written word.

Redundancy

My *American Heritage Dictionary of the English Language* defines the word *redundant* as (1) exceeding what is necessary or natural; superfluous; (2) needlessly repetitive; verbose. Doctoral dissertation writers have an

> **Tip**
>
> Organize deadlines with your advisor. Select dates upon which you will provide drafts of Chapters Four and Five. Select a date by which you will present a completed dissertation draft. Make these dates realistic. This conversation alerts your advisor to your need for attention. This conversation serves as a motivator for you to make the dissertation a top priority.

uncanny attraction to redundancy. One finds the same language in Chapter One, Chapter Three, Chapter Four, and Chapter Five to describe the research purpose, the research questions, and sometimes the research methods. This is not necessary, and you should avoid a needless repetition at all costs. This does not mean that as you write

> ### Tip
>
> If you have not done so, now may be the time to check all verbs in the first three sections of the dissertation. If at first you drafted a proposal describing what you intended to do, now you have done it. Thus, verbs that were in a future tense need to be changed to verbs in the past tense.

Chapters Four and Five that you avoid all reference to what you set out to do. It means that you don't have to repeat word for word the sections where you conveyed purpose and questions and method.

Summary of Findings

It is a good idea to end this chapter with a summary of your findings. Often Chapter Four contains a great deal of information, sometimes highly technical information. You will add to clarity if you provide a concise summary of what you found out at the conclusion of this chapter. And, of some importance, such a summary will provide you with a good lead or transition into the next chapter in which you discuss the results.

6

The Concluding Section

What did you learn? What does it mean? What did you not learn? Of what significance are your findings? Can you make any suggestions for future research or for practice? In this chapter, you have the opportunity to think creatively about your study and help the reader interpret the data and information you have already presented. It is also the chapter in which you build a case for the importance of your study. There is also an order you can follow in building this final chapter. Conventional sections of this chapter include the following:

1. A reminder of your purpose and question

2. A discussion of your findings

3. An assessment of the significance of your findings

4. A list of recommendations for practice of future research

As is usually the case, it makes sense to provide an overview of this chapter at its beginning. Offer a brief summary of what you will cover in it. This will help you by providing an outline to follow.

A Discussion of Your Findings

All writing is ultimately a question of solving a problem.

—W. Zinsser, 1990, p. 59

For many students, this part of the dissertation proves to be the most enjoyable. At this point, you make sense of the data that you have gathered as you attempt to answer the questions with which you began. As Zinsser suggests, now your writing is a question of solving a problem. In this case, the problem is what does it all mean? It is usually appropriate to begin this chapter with a recapitulation of the purpose and questions. Remind the reader what you set out to do. But do not be redundant in doing so. There is no need to repeat everything you have said earlier.

Next, give meaning to your data. Were you able to answer your research questions and, if so, how good an answer did you provide? It is ironic that at this point of the dissertation, when many sets of eyes are better than one set of eyes, the doctoral student usually is the only one trying to understand the data. Using the dissertation support group that is discussed elsewhere in this book can lessen some of the liability associated with solo scholarship. Having others look at your data can be a very rewarding activity and may lead to discovery. If you are interacting with peers via e-mail or a chat room, it helps to provide short summaries of what you are writing. Often, long attached files pose a problem for people with busy schedules and their own needs. Try to cut to the core meaning as you interpret your data.

Your advisor may take on this role of helping you interpret your data. Sending file attachments if you are communicating at a distance is helpful. But remember to help your advisor by providing summaries of what you are thinking.

If your study is a quantitative study exploring relationships between and among variables, this is the section where you discuss the significance of what you found. "What you found" was presented in Chapter Four. In this chapter, you discuss the meaning of those results. Statistics do not usually come in black and white. Statistical results of various strengths need to be explored and discussed. Regression coefficients need to be explained. Remember that findings of nonsignificance need to be discussed as well. Talk about your results.

If your study is a qualitative study, this is where you discuss the themes that you have found. Normally, the presentation of the themes was accomplished in Chapter Four. In this chapter, you discuss the implications and meanings of these themes. Often, in this chapter the writer weaves the work of other scholars into the construction of meaning. In fact, in some qualitative studies, it is in the discussion of the meaning of the data that other scholarship takes on much significance.

Eisner (1991) offers much excellent advice on interpreting and understanding qualitative data (or text). One of Eisner's points is that researchers should be concerned with what makes their qualitative data believable. He suggests that coherence, consensus, and instrumental utility can serve as a guide for evaluating such data (1991, p. 53). I recommend that you look carefully in selected qualitative texts for advice about interpreting qualitative data.

> **Tip**
>
> Sometimes advisors encourage the doctoral scholar to consider writing the final chapter as an article for publication in a scholarly journal. In this case, the final chapter will be a highly condensed report of the purpose, question, important literature, method, findings, and recommendations of the dissertation. The chapter will be prepared in keeping with the editorial requirements of a target academic journal.

I should note also that the conventions I have presented relative to Chapter Five are not always useful for the student carrying out a qualitative study. At times, the presentation of data (Chapter Four), the discussion of data (Chapter Five), and the creative use of other scholarship (Chapter Two) are woven together in an ending chapter. For the nontraditional student who develops an alternative scheme for presenting the dissertation study, make sure that your advisor supports this different format. But please realize that you have ample room to write your study according to your own design.

An Assessment of the Significance of Your Findings

Doubt is an important ingredient in any meaningful enterprise.

—John Redhead, 2002

What happens if I don't find anything of significance or if nothing in particular comes out of my qualitative study? Most of us begin a research project with the expectation that we will be able to answer our research question(s) with some new contribution to how things work. When our statistical tests do not reach significance or when we simply can't find any clear set of themes in our qualitative data, we may be disappointed. The truth is that most dissertations do not result in findings that reshape the world.

The healthiest way to approach this section of your work is to follow Redhead's advice and begin with doubt. How probable is it that what you did or did not discover is in fact true? It is difficult to attribute significance to findings if there is a serious question about the veracity of those findings. You may also wish to approach your findings from the perspective of possibility: If what I discovered is in fact the case, then here are the implications of such a finding.

Using the Concept of Type I/Type II Errors

Some dissertations seek mainly to describe. Other dissertations are searches for significance, for some kind of evidence that will bring about improvements in practice or performance. It is useful to reflect on the design of the quantitative study in speaking about findings. If you found nothing significant or remarkable, it is possible that you missed an important relationship. It is possible that you did not miss anything, too. In statistical language, this is the problem of the Type I error (you erred in missing a finding of significance or in retaining a null hypothesis of no difference). Many doctoral dissertations deal with small cases or small numbers, so it is entirely possible that, had the student the resources to do a much larger study, a more robust finding might have resulted. If you did find some significant result, it is possible that you are in error in the opposite manner. In statistical language, this is the problem of the Type II error (you erred in accepting your significant finding when it is, in fact, false). Scholars tend to be more critical when a study leads to a finding of significance because such findings often lead to calls to action. Others may do things based on your findings that might lead to harm.

It is a useful strategy in an oral defense and, for that matter, in any presentation of research to consider the factors that might cause your findings to be erroneous. Consider the quality of your research design. Consider the quality of your data. If you are wrong, what factors might have caused you to err? Should you be right, what factors cause you to be cautious in asserting the correctness of your conclusions? When you make a recommendation for practice, how convinced are you that your recommendations will be of benefit. As a researcher, you have an obligation to consider limitations to your method. An additional benefit will be that a supervisory committee may be impressed with your thoughtfulness and willingness to view your own work with a degree of impartiality.

A List of Recommendations for Practice or for Future Research

It is not unreasonable to expect researchers to have something to contribute as a result of their studied detachment and inquiry-oriented perspective.

—H. Wolcott, 1990, p. 59

In the quote above, Wolcott argued for the reasonable expectation that research projects should provide some sort of helpful reflection or advice for practitioners. The completed dissertation joins a family of scholarly work. As a member of that community, the researcher usually indicates how the dissertation study can contribute to scholarship by suggesting areas of needed future research. Because education and the social sciences often have a direct relationship to professional practice, it is quite common for dissertation researchers to also connect their findings to ways to improve practice.

But, all conclusions and recommendations must be based on the data or evidence collected. A person may have a pet theory about how the world should work, but if that person has no evidence in support of that belief, the expression of that belief in a conclusion or recommendation should wait for a later time. It is common for supervisory committees to ask the student to rework the final chapter because the student has made recommendations that cannot be supported by the data of the study. The dissertation convention requires the reporting of only those recommendations that can be logically drawn from the data. One of the last activities of most dissertation advisors is to make sure that what is reported to the scholarly community via the published abstract can be supported.

Summary

This chapter has presented you with ideas for dealing with your data once you have it assembled. For the nontraditional student, I cannot overemphasize the importance of having a peer group or some other individuals with whom you can discuss your findings. This act will add richness to your study.

7

Sage Advice on Navigating the Dissertation Process

The last chapter of this book addresses a number of topics that are frequently broached in dissertation proposal classes. Some of these topics are of relevance to all students. Some are of particular interest to the nontraditional student. Realize that doctoral programs vary from campus to campus. For example, not all programs require an oral defense of the proposal and of the actual dissertation; some require only an oral defense of the proposal. Not all programs locate final authority with the supervisory committee; some have college or institutional oversight committees that must approve dissertation research. But, the items I discuss below have frequently been matters of concern for students, nontraditional and traditional alike.

Understanding the Supervisory Committee

Graduate students in general, but especially doctoral students, are in highly vulnerable positions. They often believe their entire career rests upon not only completing the degree, but on obtaining the high regard of their professors. They are not far wrong.

—Elliot Eisner, 1991, p. 240

If Columbus had an advisory committee, he would probably still be at the dock.

—Justice Arthur Goldberg*

No matter what Justice Goldberg thought about advisory committees, such committees are, as Eisner observed, a fact of life for doctoral students. The nontraditional student neglects the supervisory committee at his or her peril. But, it is important to realize that the supervisory committee is not an antagonist. Its members are interested in your success. Supervisory committee members tend to be task oriented and they come together only at episodic moments in your program: to approve your program of studies, to approve your comprehensive examination, to approve your dissertation proposal, and to approve your dissertation. It is not always this way. Sometimes the committee takes an active role in some scholarly initiative with the student. Generally, however, the committee convenes itself rarely.

How committees are formed differs from institution to institution. On some campuses, the supervisory committee is formed or reformed when the student becomes a candidate and is working on the dissertation research study. On others, the committee is formed upon entry into the doctoral program and remains the supervisory committee throughout the program. In all instances, doctoral supervisory committees arise from the political turf of graduate colleges and their faculty.

The work of administering a doctoral program requires that the faculty share in spreading the supervisory load around. Accordingly, many faculty members have established relationships with other faculty colleagues with whom they trade off the workload. Your committee will no doubt reflect some of this in terms of both its composition and which members are asked to carry out which duties. Accordingly, the behavior of individual faculty members may be influenced by past concessions and by present needs. There is a great deal of implicit political trading that occurs. One will, for example, acquiesce to the need of a faculty colleague, cognizant of the high probability that one will want a favor from that person at some point in the future. Clearly, the doctoral candidate wants a supervisory committee that functions effectively within this political climate.

Supervisory committee members also function as part of a research community. The members bring their own disciplinary biases to their supervisory roles. They bring the culture of their academic departments to their supervisory role. Lacking a sustained exposure to these biases and cultures, the nontraditional student may not fully understand how powerful these forces can be as an influence on the actions of the supervisory committee.

How does the nontraditional student relate to the supervisory committee? Nontraditional students have options. In many places, the student will travel to the campus for meetings with the supervisory committee. But faculty members also now organize other types of meetings:

1. Conference calls

2. Video conferencing

3. Synchronous online meetings

In some programs, faculty members have relaxed the rules that govern their operating procedures as members of supervisory committees. For example, on some campuses, advisors sometimes take on a more active role in distributing work from the student to the rest of the committee with requests for input or approval. What used to require a face-to-face meeting now is accomplished by memorandum and e-mail communication. A student's dissertation proposal may be approved without a meeting of the committee. Members read it and react. When all are satisfied with the proposal, the chair is told to permit the student to proceed. Some oral defenses are conducted just as proposal meetings are conducted, using phones or conferencing technology. On the other hand, the modus operandi of the supervisory committee may remain dependent upon campus visits. The nontraditional student needs to understand how the committee will function.

There are other functions performed by your committee. When you and your chairperson feel your dissertation is ready to go to your committee, the chairperson usually selects committee members (often two other individuals from your committee) to serve as readers. That selection may be made based on which member is most likely to have appropriate knowledge of your work. But, the selection may also be made based on which member your chairperson feels comfortable asking to take on the task of reading your study. Once readers have been selected and have your study in hand, it will take close to a month (unless it is over the summer) for you to hear anything back from them.

If you should encounter problems with a member of your committee, don't wait to speak to your advisor. Even if you suspect your advisor will be unsympathetic, don't wait. If you avoid your advisor, and if you end up in a difficult situation with a particular member, you will have made matters worse. In many doctoral programs, once faculty members are appointed to a supervisory committee, they can be removed only with their own consent. But, since virtually every faculty member has an ample allotment of doctoral work, a request to have a replacement on a committee is usually not a problem. Be aware, also, that the supervisory committee with which you begin may not be the same committee at the end. Students customarily experience changes in the membership of their committees.

> **Tip**
>
> If you face a severe time crunch in terms of collecting data, alert your committee to this need. For example, if you are collecting data from subjects who are nine-month workers in public schools, you will need to do so when school is in session. Let your committee members know if you face such a time bind.

What was said about familiarizing yourself with your advisor's work also applies to your committee. Educate yourself about the writings and professional lives of your committee members.

Luminaries

Every path has its puddle.

—Anonymous*

In most fields, there are some individuals who, by virtue of their work, have become highly prominent. It is probable that there are such scholars in your field. One of the interesting aspects of being a doctoral student at work on a dissertation is that most of these prominent scholars will want to assist you. Thus, if there are leading scholars or luminaries who have written powerful and persuasive articles or books about your topic, you may wish to contact these individuals with questions. Because most faculty in most research universities now use e-mail and often have Web sites, locating these individuals is not always difficult. You should not be hesitant to contact any researcher with questions or requests for advice. Most scholars are delighted when doctoral students take an interest in their work and will be responsive to questions. You should probably make sure that the questions you ask are built on the foundation of your own knowledge. Don't ask for help if you don't know what it is that you really want. Contacting such individuals may be of special help to the nontraditional student who may not have access to ready information about present research activities. The message is: Don't be shy about calling important people.

The Proposal Meeting

Proposal defenses usually don't last more than two excruciating hours.

—Fitzpatrick, Secrist, & Wright, 1998, p. 16

The proposal meeting is usually a positive and supportive meeting. To be sure, your study is the center of attention and your committee is looking critically at it. But these meetings are seldom adversarial. Your committee will want you to have a well-designed study. You should hope to end this meeting with an understood contract of what you must do to complete your degree and a collective understanding of how you will carry out the plan. Be prepared to answer these questions about your study:

What am I going to study?

Why do I wish to study this topic?

How will I study this topic?

What might I contribute as a consequence of this study?

Overheads do help, but the best presentation of a research study I ever witnessed was one in which the student stood before the committee and spoke with great clarity and passion for about half an hour with only his verbal and nonverbal skills at work. Many students like to use a computer program such as PowerPoint. Keep slides or overheads to a minimum. Typical material in visuals might include a few sentences about purpose, a visual of your research questions, a graphic or map of your literature review, and a graphic of your design. Remember when making visuals that large print is good—18-point font or higher. Do not put too much text in a visual. If you do use a software program, make sure that your technology is working before the meeting, and provide yourself with hard copies in the event that some aspect of your technology fails. Nontraditional students are finding that video conferencing can work. Some present their proposals or defend their studies via Web-based conferencing.

You are ready to have the proposal meeting when your chairperson says so. You also know this when you are able to respond to all queries and questions with clear, definite, and confident responses. As I have said elsewhere, establishing that confidence about your dissertation means having conversations about your study with others. The more you have to explain what you want to do and how you want to do it, the more you will gain in clarity, focus, and confidence. It is very important to have that confidence for your meeting to propose your study.

There is a disquieting thing that sometimes happens at proposal meetings. Your dissertation is suddenly at risk of becoming something other than what you proposed to do. There are times when, in critiquing what you propose, a committee member discovers a different study. In such a case, your study becomes the study of one of your committee members. That is, during the examination of your proposal, a committee member suggests a study with a different twist. I experienced such an event recently. A student proposed to do a logistic regression analysis of whether a diagnostic test predicted certain probable results on a professional licensure examination. The diagnostic test was given as part of a test-preparation course. One committee member thought that the student should study the efficacy of the preparation course, not the power of the diagnostic test used. This suggestion constituted a very different dissertation. Fortunately, a strong chair and another wise committee member were able to intervene and block the proposed change. The student could also have done this by saying, "That would be another study and it is not the one I want to do." Be prepared to make such a statement. Of course, to make such a statement, you have to have your own study clearly in your mind.

In both the proposal meeting and the oral defense, there are strategic issues. Should you provide summaries or copies of overheads in addition to the written proposal or draft? Should you stand

and talk or sit? Can guests be invited? Should food and drink be included? What happens if a committee member has to be absent? Do you assume that everyone has read the study? These are excellent questions. The best approach to dealing with them is to ask your advisor. Usually that individual will be able to clear up all confusion over what to do and what is likely to happen at the proposal meeting or at the oral defense.

I want to note that, on many campuses, supervisory committees are beginning to expect that an institutional review board (IRB) application will accompany the proposal. If you are doing a study that involves a vulnerable population of subjects, it will be very important that your committee be able to evaluate the procedures you plan to use to protect these subjects and comply with IRB regulations.

Here is what I usually say to students who ask me such questions about the meeting. In terms of how you present your study, I think it is important to stay within your comfort range. If you do not like technology, don't use it. There is no rule that says committee members want electronic presentations. If you do use technology, plan for it not to work. You have enough to think about without falling to pieces if you can't get the technology to work. Simply resort to overheads or handouts. As I indicated above, you want to be organized and clear in presenting your study. Practice presenting your study with a group of critical friends. Even if it seems highly artificial, and perhaps unnecessary, practice presenting your study. Most of us find flaws in such a presentation. Pay obsessive attention to small details. If you do, you will be more in control when you present your study and that is what you want.

I encourage students to think strategically about the arrangement of the room. You do want to be the focal point. Position yourself accordingly. Do arrive ahead of time. Your committee members usually occupy a conference table and guests, if invited, usually do not sit directly at that table. As I have noted, it is now possible to use video streaming or Web-based conferencing as the medium for such meetings. In these instances, one is linking two physical places together through cameras and broadcasting the images of the individuals in those rooms. Technology is also now beginning to be used to broadcast the images of multiple users. In the latter instance, this would permit committee members in different locations to participate in a virtual conference with the student. In some instances, higher education institutions may have video conferencing available, and such systems can work well and save all involved time and money.

The Defense

The play was a great success, but the audience was a disaster.

—Oscar Wilde*

In most programs, the faculty expect the graduate student to present his or her study to the supervisory committee. This event is often referred to as the oral defense. The implications of this label are obvious. The student is expected to report on his or her findings and to provide a reasonably persuasive case that the findings are justified. For most students, the oral defense is a high-stakes test that produces great anxiety. And, to be sure, your supervisory committee is an audience of sorts and you want to make sure your "play" does not become a "disaster." In practice, most doctoral students successfully pass this challenge because by the time of the oral defense, committee members have paid close attention to the written draft of the dissertation. Were there a big problem with the study, it is likely that problem would have surfaced before the oral defense.

Still, it is wise to be well prepared for the defense and to be able to read the danger signals. Most defenses take place on campus, although, as I have said, technology is beginning to make itself felt, and some faculty are beginning to use phone or video conferencing. The typical format is for the doctoral candidate to make an oral presentation. The committee listens and interjects with questions. At the conclusion, the student is asked to leave the room and the committee votes on whether to accept the oral defense and approve the dissertation.

What does being prepared for the oral defense mean? First, it means having a plausible answer for every question asked. This is one reason why a dissertation support group is so invaluable. During a sustained period of interaction with others about your dissertation, you will be queried about many if not all of the decisions you made. Why did you elect this approach? Why did you phrase the questions in the way that you did? Why was your particular method the right method? How do you account for this finding? Can you really make this recommendation based on your data? Do your data really allow you to answer your questions? An endless list of potential questions surrounds your study.

Second, being prepared means speaking with confidence about your study. It can also mean being able to say that you did not consider a particular angle but you have reasons for doing what you did do. This does not mean you wish to be indifferent to suggestions. It does mean you need to defend what you did. Remember that you would not be at the point of the oral defense if your study were without merit.

Third, being prepared means speaking with clarity. Be clear. Being prepared may mean being able to report without chagrin that you really didn't find much. Do not go into an oral defense without a carefully constructed outline of what you want to say and how you want to say it. Some like to use handouts; some like to use overheads; some like to use PowerPoint or a comparable technology. Some candidates like to simply talk about their study. Be comfortable with your form of presentation. If you provide your committee with a handout, it is likely that they will look at it rather than at you. It is also common for the members of your committee to browse through their copy of your study as you talk. Do not be disconcerted by this. It means, usually, that your comments have triggered a thought they may wish to pursue once you are finished with your presentation.

Many professors have a question or two they ask of every doctoral candidate no matter the topic. Some common and generic questions heard at oral defenses include the following:

1. If you could do it over, what would you do differently?

2. How did you guard against your own biases (assuming you intended to attain some degree of objectivity in reporting your findings)?

3. In doing your study, did anything surprise you?

4. What do you intend to do with your research now that you have completed it?

5. What was the most difficult element of the study for you?

Realize also that scheduling the defense requires advance planning. Orchestrating the schedules of multiple professors is no mean trick. Thus, if you are facing a rapidly approaching institutional deadline, you or your chair may find it difficult to schedule an oral defense. Be surprised if things happen quickly but be prepared for matters to move along at a snail's pace. It is not unusual for a committee member to be absent at the meeting. When that happens, that professor usually will have indicated to the chairperson the concerns or issues he or she wishes to have raised at the meeting.

Finally, think carefully through the arrangements for this important meeting with your supervisory committee. You may or may not have responsibility for helping to make room arrangements for this meeting. Usually, you will not have to worry about scheduling a room if your meeting is on the campus or worry about teleconferencing procedures if the meeting will be done from afar. You do want to worry about yourself. If the meeting is on campus, make sure you know where the room is and what equipment will be provided. If you are videoconferencing from a distance, have a fall-back plan if the system doesn't work. You might, for example, distribute materials in advance (in addition to your dissertation draft) and use a phone conference as the means of conducting your defense. Or, you may simply have a fall-back plan that entails a visit to the campus to make your defense. If you plan to use technology in making your presentation, have it set up and working before the meeting begins. Remember the ever-lurking presence of Murphy's Law—if it can go wrong, it probably will.

Issues With Completion

I'd rather face it like a wise man should and train for ill and not for good.

—A. E. Housman, 1931

There are many things that get in the way of finishing the degree. Based on watching many students over many years, I would rate the failure to accord the proposal the second priority in one's life after family as the most common obstacle. It takes perseverance to complete the proposal and degree. The dissertation pathway is different for each person. No longer can one enjoy the comfort of a schedule that is laid out by others, by a professor, or by a program of studies. The dissertation requires internal motivation and a constant adherence to an objective. If you allow yourself to be buffeted about by all of those forces that make demands on your time, you soon finds the dissertation sliding into a place of neglect. This can be avoided by laying out a schedule and sticking to it.

Below are some commonly listed obstacles as identified by dissertation advisors with whom I have interacted:

Proposal Obstacles

Unclear focus
Undoable study
Lack of commitment
Lack of knowledge of research design
Lack of knowledge about statistics
Lack of understanding about proposal design

Personal Obstacles

A move
Health
Conflict
Money issues
Job pressure
Family pressure
Lack of perseverance
Inability to work independently
Problem with internal motivation

I will note that students who face one or more of the obstacles above can help themselves immeasurably by being clear and open with their advisors. Students enter the program at one point in time. Things change. Adult life means that a person often answers to many masters.

It is also true that if a student lacks necessary abilities, there are solutions to such problems as well. If a student is a poor writer, the student can find help with writing. If the student has a poor grasp of the methodology, the student can learn what needs to be learned. If a student has a learning disability and both conceptualization and writing pose challenges, a discussion with the advisor and the committee can help the student to find ways of surmounting such challenges. If the student has pressing personal needs, the program can be legitimately put on hold. Appendix D contains a list of dissertations that have focused on the retention and completion issues of doctoral students. If you wish to learn more about what fellow doctoral students have learned about successful completion, browse through some of the titles in this appendix.

I have known many life situations that have made it necessary for students who have completed their coursework to "stop out." The death of loved ones, sickness and disease, a suddenly overwhelming work-life, or a move from one state to another are all compelling reasons why some doctoral students have to put their dissertations on hold. If some personal need is causing you to reorder what is necessary and important to you, make sure that you speak with your advisor. Furthermore, I suggest that you communicate your situation to your whole committee. Faculty advisors of adult students are no strangers to the tragedies and demands that unfortunately impact their adult students. Communicating is far better than simply disappearing.

The faculty and the administrators of graduate programs have granted many students extensions of time to complete the study when they are alerted to individual need. Hence, if some obstacle leaps in front of you, your first step is to let people know this has happened. Make sure you understand the time constraints that will be imposed.

If you do stop out, recognize that you will inevitably experience difficulty in reestablishing your place. The little quote that began this section from the British poet, A. E. Houseman, captures the preferred behavior. Plan for ill and be pleasantly surprised if your reentry is without travail. You do need to realize that most institutions are not particularly attuned to helping students who stop out for great stretches of time. Graduate advisors may have retired or moved on to other institutions. Curricular content may well have become outdated. Research methodology will have grown in sophistication. There are many reasons why it makes sense for doctoral students to complete their dissertations and degrees within a limited time frame.

Scholars have studied the obstacles to the completion of the doctoral degree. If this interests you, Tinto (1993), Bean (1980), Golde (1994, 1996, 1998, 2000), Kember (1981, 1989), and Kember, Murphy, Siaw, and Yuen (1991) have explored the factors that impede progress and completion.

Health Issues

The body never lies.

—Martha Graham*

Health issues deserve a special note. Adults write dissertations. Illness strikes adults in many different ways. Doctoral students experience serious illnesses at times; their family members experience serious illnesses at times. It is often impossible for the student to work on a dissertation while combating an illness. As an advisor, I have had students who had to cope with cancer, with the death of parents or children, with serious medical operations, and with divorce and its attendant psychological trauma. At times, combined with the dissertation requirements, these pressures are simply unbearable. As I note above, students should alert their chair to problems that are causing difficulty.

Doctoral dissertation writing is also a sedentary activity. The Chinese have a saying: *Too much sit down break pants.* Your mind will work better if you keep your body fit. Take this advice to heart and don't neglect to fit exercise into your routine. You will think and write better as a consequence.

Dissertations, in order to be written, require that routines be adjusted. For the nontraditional student, this normally means finding time to write along with many other obligations and responsibilities. Stress is one result. Getting up very early or staying up very late can lead to health problems. Worry and anxiety can lead to health problems. Many students gain weight because food becomes a psychological crutch used as a reward or motivational tool or both. Recognize what is going on if you resort to such psychological ploys to help you work on your study. Try to find antidotes. I will repeat that exercise is one of the best.

Giving Up/Sticking It Out/Time Out

> *Will I hear the dog, now that I am unleashed*
> *For weekend walks in the woods,*
> *Bark and whistle with joy?*
>
> —M. Bryant, *On Promotion,* unpublished poem, 2002

Sometimes students face the very difficult decision about whether to continue with their program. There are many issues that impact whether a student should drop out of a doctoral program at the ABD (all but dissertation) stage. It is no easy matter to abandon the doctoral degree. Often that probability sneaks up on a person. A person finishes the coursework, passes a comprehensive examination, and starts to work on a dissertation. Life intervenes—family, job, and commitments. The doctoral dissertation fades in order of importance. Eventually enough time has passed so that a person simply cannot sustain the energy or find the time and interest to restore the dissertation to a top priority.

If you elect to abandon the degree, it will probably be a decision into which you grow. That is, life is full of many paths and not every one needs to lead to a doctoral degree. It can be and often is a very liberating experience for a doctoral candidate to come to the realization that other things are more important. If this should happen to you, savor the liberation. It is healthy and wise to recognize that you do not want the degree. I have known some that have intentionally and consciously arrived at the decision to devote their scarce time to something other than the imprimatur of an academic institution. They may wrestle with this for a while, but they eventually recognize what is important in their lives. Or, at least that is what I think based on my observations of those who have struggled with this decision.

Publishing From Your Dissertation

Res ipsa loguitur (the thing speaks for itself)

—Latin saying

In some disciplines, there is an expectation that a person will be able to publish two to four articles from his or her dissertation. Some individuals publish their dissertations as books. Some publish major sections of their dissertations as books. It is worth contemplating publishing from your study. After all, you have done a study. It has something to say; let it speak.

Your dissertation is your book. It will be bound as a book and placed in your institution's library. The abstract of your study will be available through *Dissertation Abstracts,* and those who wish to order a copy of your study may read it on microfiche or hard copy. But there is the potential for a wider audience for your study if you publish academic papers or a book. There are two parts of the typical dissertation that can be transformed into an academic paper: (1) the literature review and (2) the findings and recommendations. If you have done a good job with your literature review, it is quite feasible that you might wish to rework this into an article on your topic. If you would seek some models of this type of article, a search through the editions of *Educational Research,* a monthly publication of the American Educational Research Association (AERA), will be helpful. You should also be cognizant of the journals in your area of interest. Make sure you understand the expectations of the editors in terms of style, length, and format.

A second part of the typical dissertation that can be converted to an academic paper is the section detailing your question(s) and the answers you found to your question(s) and their implications. That is, you set out to gather information about a topic or issue of some importance. Sharing your findings with the research community is important. This is true, even if you are not embarking on or continuing an academic career. I encourage everyone to develop a research article from the study and to publish it. Glatthorn (2002) has written a book called *Publish or Perish: The Educator's Imperative.* He offers many helpful suggestions of a concrete nature for becoming a professional writer.

A usual first step on the road to publication is to prepare a paper for a presentation at a scholarly conference. If you do, I recommend that you include the following sections: introduction, background, research question, theoretical framework, design, findings, and recommendations. Usually proposals for conferences are brief—three to four pages. Many such conferences now require online proposals, so be sure to check to see if there is such a process in place. The divisions of the AERA, for example, now provide for electronic submissions.

Publishing with your advisor, a member of your supervisory committee, or a research team poses particular issues about which you will wish to be aware.

Proofreading

> *Get the little book! Get the little book! Get the little book!*
>
> —E. B. White in Strunk and White, 1959, p. xii

One of the disquieting events almost all doctoral recipients experience occurs at a point some months or even years after the completion of the study. The researcher rereads the study and usually is mildly horrified at the number of grammatical and syntactical errors that appear. After many drafts and multiple sets of readers, it will appear strange that so many errors still exist. At least, this is true for many dissertations. You, the researcher, must accept responsibility for a close reading of the final draft.

Acknowledgment Page

> *Let the fall leaves fall and the cold snow snow*
> *And the rain rain rain 'til April*
> *Our coats are warm and the pantry's full*
> *And there's cake upon the table.*
>
> —Watson, 1971

The little poem above is a great comfort. The words told my kids at nighttime readings that all is right with the world. When you write this part of your dissertation, you have completed a great challenge. Many of us feel this comfort almost physically. Speak about your gratitude. There is cake upon your table. Take delight in that reality.

It is both convention and wisdom to include in your dissertation a page or two where you acknowledge those who have contributed to your success. Spouses, children, loved ones, good friends, committee members, teachers old and new, sometimes even a pet may have provided support along the way. Your advisor will have played an important role. Think about how you write this. Read what other students have written to give you a sense of the convention. Then, write your own. Those who know you will read this. It is your special communication to special people.

Attending Graduation

I am a part of all that I have met.

—Alfred Lord Tennyson*

Attending graduation is almost always a matter of choice. You don't have to go. Sometimes distance is a great obstacle. Sometimes a job does not permit attendance. Still, if possible, attending the graduation ceremony is good for you and good for your family and friends. As Lord Tennyson observed, we are part of all that which we have met. You are a part of the institution that grants you your degree. You are a part of the scholarly community that provided the program in which you studied. You are part of many communities. This is one of the few times in your life when you can bring those diverse communities together in celebration.

I like graduation ceremonies. They honor those who have labored and earned recognition. They bring closure to a period of sustained effort and serve to mark the end of one chapter and the beginning of another. Ceremonies are also a good way to put to rest the type of letdown or postpartum experience of no longer working on the degree. After the dissertation is finished and one no longer needs to adjust one's life to the study, it is common to feel a sense of disorientation and depression. The graduation ceremony can be a salve to this sore. Graduation ceremonies are also ways to cement continued relationships with peers that hopefully have become valuable to you.

Celebrating together can become one of those memories you will always cherish.

Going to graduation is a good thing to do.

The Doctoral Hood and Gown

Your doctoral gown symbolizes your membership in the scholarly community of your discipline. Seize every opportunity life presents to wear it with pride.

—M. Bryant, A speech at the University of Nebraska-Lincoln Doctoral hooding ceremony, May 2001

As you will discover, once you have earned your degree you are entitled to wear a gown and doctoral hood that is a historic part of academic traditions. While some may be tempted to avoid ceremony and pomp, the wearing of the doctoral regalia at ceremonies is an honor to which you are entitled. Such ceremony brings many benefits to you and to educational organizations. You can purchase your gown, your hood, and mortarboard, although these will be expensive. When I last looked at one of the national distributors of such regalia, the price for a faculty gown, hood, and mortarboard ranged from $350.00 to $450.00 depending on the options chosen. If you are anticipating many opportunities to wear these robes, it is worthwhile to purchase them. If you own your hood and gown, you will remove from your path an obstacle that may block participation in ceremonies, such as the task of renting a gown and hood. Besides, when you think about the labor you put into attaining the privilege, the purchase price may not seem so steep.

If you are not likely to be participating in academic ceremonies, then you will be wiser and richer by not purchasing the doctoral regalia. Should you need to wear these robes for some occasion, you can find them at businesses that rent these at commencement ceremonies all over the country.

Final Words

I began this discussion of dissertation writing for the nontraditional student with the metaphor of climbing a mountain. I will end with another reflection drawing upon mountains and climbers. Rene Daumal, a French mountaineer, wrote this reflection.

You cannot stay on the summit forever. You have to come down again. So why bother in the first place? Just this: what is above knows what is below. What is below knows not what is above. One climbs, one sees, one descends, one sees no longer. But one has seen. There is an art in conducting one's self in the lower regions by the memory of what one has seen higher up. When one can no longer see, one can at least know.

—R. Daumal, 1971

Once you have finished climbing your mountain, you will understand the truthfulness of what Daumal says to us. You will know more about yourself and others. You will know more about how things work. I encourage you to reflect on what you have seen during your climb and to remember this knowledge as you move into the next chapter of your life and career.

Appendix A

Annotated Bibliography of Useful Books

Below is a list of useful books on various aspects of methodology. The nontraditional student should be alert to texts that promise to be of use in developing the methodology. Many are available from educational publishers that specialize in methods texts. Before purchasing these books sight unseen, a student would be wise to visit a library and examine those that appear of interest. The titles below are, for the most part, ones that I know to be popular with dissertation writers.

Very Useful Books of a General Nature

Fitzpatrick, J., Secrist, J., & Wright, D. (1998). *Secrets for a successful dissertation.* Thousand Oaks, CA: Sage.

These three authors recount their experiences as dissertation writers. Full of good humor and sensible advice, this book should be a good companion for you as you travel through the stages of the dissertation process.

Glatthorn, A. (1998). *Writing the winning dissertation: A step-by-step guide.* Thousand Oaks, CA: Corwin.

This book covers a wide array of topics related to writing dissertations. It is a good source for information about dissertation conventions in general.

Locke, L., Spirduso, W., & Silverman, S. (2000). *Proposals that work: A guide for planning dissertations and grant proposals.* Thousand Oaks, CA: Sage.

These authors use a broad brush to discuss many topics in the creation and writing of research studies and grant proposals. I find their book particularly helpful with quantitative studies, but they cover many other topics as well. They also provide many examples of how to carry out a research project.

***Publication Manual of the American Psychological Association* (5th ed.). (2001).** Washington, DC: American Psychological Association (APA).

This style guide has become the bible for doctoral students in the social sciences and education. Unless your advisor instructs you to use a different style guide, buy this book. It helps you with all phases of a dissertation, from tips on writing, to presenting information in graphs and tables, to how to format your citations.

Rossman, M. (2002). *Negotiating graduate school.* Thousand Oaks, CA: Sage.

Drawing on his experience advising many doctoral students, the author presents a host of topics that concern most doctoral students. For the person just beginning a program, Rossman's book has the utility of laying out the pieces of doctoral work. It is a good book to use to help you know what questions to ask about your own program.

Rudestam, K. E., & Newton, R. R. (1992). *Surviving your dissertation.* Thousand Oaks, CA: Sage.

Of particular interest in this book is a section on Presenting the Results of Empirical Studies. Although some of the examples offered are a bit out of date with current APA recommendations, there are many useful strategies presented by these two authors relative to how to present data and to organize the chapter of the dissertation dealing with the actual data collected by the researcher.

Books on Quantitative Methods

Below are books that offer useful technical advice about a wide range of quantitative research topics. At the end of this section on quantitative resources, I include a few sources for instruments and scales that may be of use.

Babbie, E. (1990). *Survey research methods* (2nd ed.). Belmont, CA: Wadsworth.

Babbie's book remains one of the classic works on survey research. His discussion of different forms of longitudinal survey studies is excellent. The detail that he provides for sampling populations is also very useful.

Borg, W., & Gall, M. (1989). *Educational research: An introduction* (5th ed.). New York: Longman.

Borg and Gall's comprehensive textbook on research in education has been used in many graduate research classes. It is a storehouse of information with a strong focus on quantitative methods.

Campbell, D., & Stanley, J. (1966). Experimental and quasi-experimental designs for research. In N. L. Gage (Ed.), *Handbook of research on teaching* (pp. 1–76). Chicago: Rand McNally.

The chapter from this book on experimental and quasi-experimental design has served to educate generations of students on quantitative design. The factors identified in this chapter that may compromise quantitative research designs should be understood by all doctoral students. When you write your section on delimitations and limitations, this chapter will help.

Creswell, J. (2003). *Research design: Qualitative, quantitative, and mixed methods approaches.* Thousand Oaks, CA: Sage.

Creswell's book, originally published in 1994, remains popular with students because the author clearly identifies different design approaches. He does this for both quantitative and qualitative designs. This updated version of the original text contains many more examples of various research approaches. In conceptualizing ways to treat dependent and independent variables and in delineating the basic qualitative approaches, it is a must for the doctoral student's library.

Fowler, F. (1988). *Survey research methods.* Newbury Park, CA: Sage.

This is a very practical presentation of survey research. Fowler provides the basic elements of carrying out a survey research project.

Gardner, R. C. (2001). *Psychological statistics using SPSS.* Upper Saddle River, NJ: Prentice Hall.

Gardner provides help for researchers wanting information about the outcomes of SPSS tests.

Green, S. B., Salkind, J. J., & Akeny, T. M. (2000). *Using SPSS for Windows: Analyzing and understanding data.* Upper Saddle River, NJ: Prentice Hall.

This is an excellent resource for those who want to be better able to understand, utilize, and write about the results of statistical tests run with SPSS. The book also covers in detail the proper way to present the output of SPSS analyses.

Isaac, S., & Michael, W. (1981). *Handbook in research and evaluation: A collection of principles, methods, and strategies useful in the planning, design, and evaluation of studies in education and the behavioral sciences* (2nd ed.). San Diego, CA: EDITS.

Addressed to an audience of professional researchers and evaluators, this book contains information about experimental designs and about design flaws.

Kazdin, A., & Tuma, A. H. (Eds.). (1982). *Single-case research design.* San Francisco: Jossey-Bass.

"Investigation of the individual subject has an extensive history in psychological research" (p. 33). This text contains a series of articles all oriented toward the assessment of performance over time, measured at a number of times with the same subject. This method is sometimes labeled *small n research.* It is also an approach that can include direct observations of performance and the "evaluation of data through visual inspection" (p. 39).

Keppel, G. (1991). *Design and analysis: A researcher's handbook* (3rd ed.). Englewood Cliffs, NJ: Prentice Hall.

For the student conducting a study using inferential statistics, this book will be helpful. Analysis of variance, regression, and path analysis are covered. The author includes approaches to calculating the necessary sample size using several different approaches.

Kerlinger, F. (1973). *Foundations of behavioral research.* New York: Holt, Rinehart, & Winston.

This book has been used in many research classes. It is a classic text in quantitative methods. If you are doing a study that involves hypothesis testing, you can benefit from a close examination of Kerlinger's text.

Nicol, A. A., & Pexman, P. M. (1999). *Presenting your findings: A practical guide for creating tables.* Washington, DC: American Psychological Association.

This is a highly recommended resource for help in creating tables using APA format. The book is available through Amazon.com for approximately $11.00.

Pedhazer, E. J. (1997). *Multiple regression in behavioral research: Explanation and predictions* (3rd ed.). Fort Worth, TX: Harcourt Brace College.

This is a technical book but will be very useful to those considering or using some form of regression analysis in analyzing the relationships between dependent and independent variables. It covers a range of regression analyses and includes sample output from various statistical packages.

Shadish, W. R., Cook, T. D., & Campbell, D. T. (2002). *Experimental and quasi-experimental designs for generalized and causal inferences.* Boston: Houghton-Mifflin.

This is a very helpful resource for those wanting to find detailed explanations and guidelines in critiquing the design issues in various quantitative research statistical and design approaches. The authors also delineate the various strengths and weaknesses of different quantitative designs. This book will help the doctoral student construct the Chapter One sections on assumptions, delimitations, and limitations.

Sources for Instruments and Scales

Bowling, A. (1999). *Measuring disease: A review of disease-specific quality of life measurement scales.* Philadelphia: Open University Press.

Bowling provides a long list of instruments related to various medical diseases and quality of life issues. She includes a discussion of many different medical conditions, from hospital anxiety to pain to quality of life issues. Researchers looking for instruments to measure medical conditions and their severity will find this resource useful.

Hauser, R. M., Brown, B. V., & Prosser, W. R. (1997). *Indicators of children's well-being.* New York: Russell Sage Foundation.

The editors present 24 separate chapters in which a chapter author reviews measuring issues and techniques focused on some aspect of the well-being of children or young adults. For example, David Koretz offers an excellent discussion of the common issues found in measuring educational achievement. Koretz includes in his discussion an enlightening critique of the National Assessment of Educational Process (NAEP). Other chapters cover childhood poverty, family structure issues, behavioral problems, and adolescent development measures.

Plake, B., Impara, J., & Spies, R. (Eds.). (2003). *The fifteenth mental measurements yearbook.* Lincoln: University of Nebraska Press.

The Buros Institute is dedicated to monitoring the quality of commercially published tests. In addition to promoting appropriate test selection, use, and practice, the Buros Institute works to encourage improved test development and research through thoughtful, critical analysis of individual instruments and the promotion of an open dialogue regarding contemporary measurement issues. The titles published by the Buros Institute are focused on providing consumers and other test users with accurate evaluations of the usefulness and effectiveness of commercially available tests.

Books on Qualitative Methods

Below are texts that are helpful in constructing qualitative methodological approaches to answering the research question.

Behar, R. (1996). *The vulnerable observer: Anthropology that breaks your heart.* Boston: Beacon.

"For me, anthropology is about embarking on just such a voyage through a long tunnel . . . the desire to enter into the world around you and having no idea how to do it, the fear of observing too coldly or too distractedly or too raggedly, the rage of cowardice, the insight that is always arriving late, as defiant hindsight, a sense of the utter uselessness of writing anything and yet the burning desire to write something" (p. 3). Behar thinks deeply about the work of the researcher who studies people and their lives. If your study is a qualitative study, I recommend you read her book.

Bogdan, R., & Biklen, S. (1992). *Qualitative research for education: An introduction to theory and methods* (2nd ed.). Boston: Allyn & Bacon.

Bogdan and Biklen have helped thousands of dissertation students with the design of qualitative studies. This book is a very useful source for information about doing qualitative work, organizing data, writing qualitative studies, using multiple methods of both data collection and presentation, building fieldnotes, and analyzing data.

Brewer, J., & Hunter, A. (1989). *Multi-method research: A synthesis of styles.* Sage Library of Social Research, Vol. 175. Newbury Park, CA: Sage.

If you would like advice about mixed methods, this book can help. You can also gain a clear understanding of the distinctions between the two schools of thought relative to research methods.

Creswell, J. (1994). *Research design: Qualitative and quantitative approaches.* Thousand Oaks, CA: Sage.

Creswell's text was mentioned above for its utility in designing quantitative studies. It serves a similar usefulness for those interested in qualitative designs, covering a variety in clear detail. Creswell's text was written expressly for doctoral students and therefore provides a one-stop shopping resource for both quantitative and qualitative designs. This text has recently been redone. The most recent edition (2003) is a very useful text and, like its earlier versions, will help many doctoral students sort through methodological alternatives.

Denzin, N., & Guba, Y. (Eds.). (1994). *Handbook of qualitative research.* Thousand Oaks, CA: Sage.

This is a comprehensive encyclopedia of qualitative research. It contains specific essays on such topics as phenomenology and case study. It is an excellent source for basic information.

Eisner, E. (1991). *The enlightened eye.* New York: MacMillan.

Eisner writes better than most. His book is a serious examination of ethnography, but it is also playful. Eisner gives many examples of how to write, including an absorbing little section on William Bennet's attempt to teach the *Federalist Papers* to a high school class. This book also contains his description of Educational Connoisseurship, an approach to program evaluation that he has advocated. For the doctoral student seeking to better understand qualitative research, Eisner provides an insider's view of the philosophical foundation of qualitative work.

Fetterman, D. (1989). *Ethnography step by step.* Applied Social Science Research Methods Series, Vol. 17. Newbury Park, CA: Sage.

This is a very clear and useful book for the person interested in learning how to gain the emic (the insider's viewpoint) perspective on a research topic. He also presents a very readable and informed discussion of theory in general. This discussion will be useful for the student considering the differences between a descriptive study and one built from a theoretical perspective.

Geertz, C. (1973). Thick description: Toward an interpretive theory of culture. In C. Geertz (Ed.), *The interpretation of culture* (pp. 3–30). New York: Basic Books.

It was Geertz that coined the term, "thick, rich description." He was one of the pioneers of qualitative research, and his chapter in this book, analyzing Indonesian culture by examining the social meaning of local cockfighting, remains one striking example of thorough qualitative research.

Geertz, C. (1988). *Works and lives: The anthropologist as author.* Stanford, CA: Stanford University Press.

Any study using qualitative methods would benefit from this work. Geertz discusses how the scholar goes about the business of interpreting research subjects and focuses on the issue of researcher objectivity.

LeCompte, M. D., & Schensul, J. J. (1999). *Designing and conducting ethnographic research.* Ethnographer's Toolkit, Vol. 1. Walnut Creek, CA: AltaMira.

This book has become a very useful guide to carrying out fieldwork and provides detailed information from the perspective of the ethnographic practitioner.

Lincoln, Y. S., & Guba, E. G. (1985). *Naturalistic inquiry.* Beverly Hills, CA: Sage.

Lincoln and Guba were among the first to articulate the special aspects of qualitative research. In this book, they identify many of the elements of qualitative research that distinguish it from other approaches.

Marshall, C., & Rossman, G. (1989). *Designing qualitative research.* Newbury Park, CA: Sage.

Marshall and Rossman wrote one of the early books designed to help doctoral students build a qualitative research project. Of particular utility is the number of data-gathering strategies they present.

Merriam, S. B. (1998). *Qualitative research and case study applications in education: Revised and expanded from case study research in education.* San Francisco: Jossey-Bass.

If you are using a case study method, this is a book you will want to read.

Miles, M. B., & Huberman, A. M. (1994). *Qualitative data analysis: A sourcebook* (2nd ed.). Thousand Oaks, CA: Sage.

This text has been used by many, many doctoral students as an aid in helping them figure out how to manage and analyze qualitative data. Miles and Huberman advocate a very meticulous and detailed data analysis procedure.

Moustakas, C. (1994). *Phenomenological research methods.* Thousand Oaks, CA: Sage.

Phenomenological research has become steadily more of a design feature in qualitative dissertations. If you plan to do a phenomeno-logical study, this is the text you want in your library.

Piantanida, M., & Garman, N. B. (1999). *The qualitative dissertation: A guide for students and faculty.* Thousand Oaks, CA: Corwin.

For scholars interested in approaching their dissertation study from a nonpositivist perspective and who seek both support and wisdom in doing qualitative research, this is an invaluable resource. I mentioned it earlier in the text, but their approach to the qualitative literature review is well worth reading.

Rossman, G. B., & Rallis, S. F. (1998). *Learning in the field: An intro-duction to qualitative research.* Thousand Oaks, CA: Sage.

These two authors write from years of experience working with doctoral students. Their perspective is full of a deep understanding of the difficulties of "learning in the field" and an appreciation of the full value of qualitative research as a way of knowing. They are particu-larly helpful in covering one of the most difficult tasks of qualitative research—the gathering of good data.

Rubin, H. J., & Rubin, I. S. (1995). *Qualitative interviewing: The art of hearing data.* Thousand Oaks, CA: Sage.

For the qualitative researcher, knowing how best to interview subjects is essential. This book, written by individuals who have extensive experience doing qualitative interviews, is very helpful. There is much anecdotal information provided by both authors about their experiences interviewing subjects.

Seale, C. (1999). *The quality of qualitative research.* Thousand Oaks, CA: Sage.

Seale's book, like that of Silverman below, gives you much practical wisdom about how to deal with the problem of validity and reliability in qualitative research.

Silverman, D. (2000). *Doing qualitative research: A practical handbook.* Thousand Oaks, CA: Sage.

Silverman's book contains a great deal of specific and helpful information. It is more a book about doing qualitative research and less a book describing various qualitative methods. The section on computer-assisted qualitative data analysis, which he labels CAQ-DAS, is very helpful. If you are interested in the properties of software like Ethnograph, NUD*IST, or Atlas, all software packages designed to help the qualitative researcher manage large amounts of qualitative data, Silverman provides you with careful and thoughtful analysis. He also teaches this material in his own qualitative research classes.

Spradley, J. (1979). *The ethnographic interview.* New York: Holt, Rinehart & Winston.

Spradley's book gives very helpful information about finding subjects or qualitative informants, about analyzing interviews, and about managing data. His main focus is on ethnographic practice, but many of his insights apply to any qualitative study.

Stake, R. (1995). *The art of case study research.* Thousand Oaks, CA: Sage.

Stake's book is another text that should be part of your library if you are using a case study method for your dissertation.

Strauss, A., & Corbin, J. (1990). *Basics of qualitative research: Grounded theory procedures and techniques.* Newbury Park, CA: Sage.

Grounded theory studies form another class of qualitative studies popular with dissertation scholars. This text is a must if you plan to conduct a grounded theory study.

Tashakkori, A., & Teddlie, C. (1998). *Mixed methodology.* Thousand Oaks, CA: Sage.

These authors begin with a clear history of the paradigm battle that was waged against research grounded in positivist thinking. They offer a chapter on methodological design issues that is almost a must read for the student designing a study. It is clear and to the point. They provide the outline of the typical methods section: (1) sample/data sources, (2) variables and their measurement, (3) procedures, and (4) data analysis techniques. The section on issues in measurement having to do with validity and reliability is excellent.

Tashakkori, A., & Teddlie, C. (2003). *Handbook on mixed methods in the behavioral and social sciences.* Thousand Oaks, CA: Sage.

This is an updated version of their earlier text.

Thomas, R. M. (2003). *Blending qualitative and quantitative research methods.* Thousand Oaks, CA: Corwin.

For scholars interested in combining qualitative and quantitative methods in their dissertation, Thomas's new book will be a valuable resource. It is full of concrete examples illustrating how both research traditions can be employed in the same study. Thomas also covers less common research approaches such as explanatory histories, biographies, and autobiographies. Thus, this book is particularly helpful for students interested in research methodologies that accommodate postmodern perspectives.

Wolcott, H. F. (1990). *Writing up qualitative research.* Newbury Park, CA: Sage.

This is a small book but invaluable to the qualitative researcher. As an active qualitative scholar, Wolcott knows the research tradition about which he writes. He speaks knowingly of the many difficulties and joys that the qualitative researcher experiences. Furthermore, his book is packed with useful advice for the qualitative scholar.

Yin, R. K. (1984). *Case study research: Design and methods.* Applied Social Research Methods Series, Vol. 5, Beverly Hills, CA: Sage.

Street Corner Society (1943) is noted by Yin as a classic example of the descriptive case study. Allison's *Essence of the Cuban Missile Crisis* (1971) is another. Yin provides many good examples as he delineates the features of the single or multiple case study. This is a book commonly used by individuals interested in case study design.

Appendix B

Bibliography of
Helpful Dissertations

This Appendix contains a list of dissertations that have examined the factors that appear to be associated with the successful completion of the doctoral degree and the dissertation. No matter your stage of doctoral study, a perusal of some of these studies would be helpful for three reasons: (1) these studies show you models of dissertations; (2) these studies serve as a heads-up relative to the difficulties you may encounter; and (3) these studies indicate the limited focus that is customary in the doctoral dissertation.

Andrieu, S. C. (1991). *The influence of background, graduate experience, aspirations, expected earning, and financial commitment on within-year persistence of students enrolled in graduate programs.* Doctoral dissertation, University of New Orleans, New Orleans, LA.

Bair, C. R. (1999). *Doctoral student attrition and persistence: A meta-synthesis.* Doctoral dissertation, Loyola University of Chicago, Chicago.

Bauer, W. C. (1997). *Pursuing the Ph.D.: Importance of structure, goal setting and advising practices in the completion of the doctoral dissertation.* Doctoral dissertation, University of California—Los Angeles.

Bishop, A. E. (1981). *The effect of fear of success on the completion of the doctorate.* Doctoral dissertation, University of Southern California, Los Angeles.

Bodian, L. H. (1987). *Career instrumentality of degree completion as a factor in doctoral student attrition.* Doctoral dissertation, University of Maryland, College Park.

Butler, J. N., Jr. (1995). *Individual and institutional factors related to successful completion of a doctoral degree in agricultural education.* Doctoral dissertation, Mississippi State University, Mississippi State.

Campbell, R. B. (1992). *A study of the completion and non-completion of the doctor of education degree in educational leadership at the University of Delaware.* Doctoral dissertation, University of Delaware, Newark.

Clark, A. T. (1980). *The influence of adult developmental processes upon the educational experiences of doctoral students.* Doctoral dissertation, Humanistic Psychology Institute, San Francisco.

Delaney, F. H., Jr. (1981). *Factors affecting attrition of successful degree completion among doctoral candidates at Boston College, 1972–1978.* Doctoral dissertation, Boston College, Boston.

Dickenson, W. C. (1983). *Factors relating to attrition from and completion of the doctoral program in educational administration from the University of Pittsburgh.* Doctoral dissertation, University of Pittsburgh, Pittsburgh, PA.

Ducette, M. O. (1990). *Variables influencing doctoral student graduate: A path analytic test of Tinto's process model.* Doctoral dissertation, State University of New York at Buffalo.

Ferrer De Valero, Y. J. (1996). *Departmental factors affecting time to degree and completion rates of doctoral students at one land grant research institution.* Doctoral dissertation, Virginia Polytechnic Institute, Blacksburg.

Hales, K. S. E. (1998). *The relationship between personality type, life events, and completion of the doctoral degree.* Doctoral dissertation, Texas A&M University at Commerce.

Hassan-Shahriari, F. Z. (1998). *An analysis of factors relating to the attrition rate of doctoral students at the dissertation level at the School of Education and Human Development of the George Washington University.* Doctoral dissertation, George Washington University, Washington, DC.

Howard, R. K. (1981). *A follow-up study of doctoral attrition in the College of Education.* Doctoral dissertation, Florida State University, Tallahassee.

Johnson, R. (2001). *The effects of co-cultural adaptation on African American doctoral student persistence at the University of Kentucky.* Doctoral dissertation, University of Kentucky, Lexington.

Karolyi, M. S. (1993). *All but dissertation: Perceptions of ABD level attrition among faculty, alumni, and ABDs in a graduate school of education at a large, public, midwestern university.* Doctoral dissertation, Kent State University, Kent, OH.

Koiner, J. H. (1992). *Relationship of the locus-of-control orientation of graduate students in education to their success in pursuing a doctorate degree.* Doctoral dissertation, Texas A&M University, College Station.

Lawson, L. G. (1985). *Doctoral student attrition: A role theory approach.* Doctoral dissertation, University of California at Santa Barbara.

Lemp, P. H. (1980). *Determinants of persistence in graduate education: The doctoral student.* Doctoral dissertation, Stanford University, Stanford, CA.

Lenz, K. S. (1994). *A multiple case study examining factors affecting the completion of the doctoral dissertation by academically able women.* Doctoral dissertation, University of Denver, Denver, CO.

Mariano, C. M. (1993). *A study of Ed.Ds, Ph.Ds, and ABDs in educational administration (dissertation completion).* Doctoral dissertation, Boston College, Boston.

Myers, L. H. (1999). *Barriers to completion of the doctoral degree in educational administration.* Doctoral dissertation, Virginia Polytechnic Institute and State University, Blacksburg.

O'bara, C. C. (1993). *Why some finish and why some don't: Factors affecting Ph.D. completion.* Doctoral dissertation, Claremont Graduate School, Claremont, CA.

O'Connell, E. C. (1991). *An investigation of the relationship of psychological type to completion of the Doctor of Philosophy degree.* Doctoral dissertation, Loyola University of Chicago.

Quinn, E. C. (1991). *Doctoral student retention and selected personal factors.* Doctoral dissertation, University of Southern Mississippi, Hattiesburg.

Reiff, M. (1992). *Adults in graduate school: A qualitative study of how experience differs for persisting and non-persisting students.* Doctoral dissertation, University of California at Santa Barbara.

Rice, L. T. (1981). *A profile of the female doctoral student who persisted to the completion of the doctoral degree.* Doctoral dissertation, Auburn University, Auburn, AL.

Rode, W. H. (1998). *Role of a learning community-based program in doctoral dissertation completion: A case study of program factors related to dissertation completion in a professional development program with an emphasis in staff development at the University of Maryland.* Doctoral dissertation, University of Maryland, College Park.

Schultz, M. C. (1983). *ABD doctoral students from off-campus centers of the University of Southern California.* Doctoral dissertation, University of Southern California, Los Angeles.

Schwarz, S. (1997), *Students' perceptions of the role of the dissertation chair in time to complete the doctoral dissertation.* Doctoral dissertation, Pennsylvania State University, University Park.

Smith, P. R. (1993). *A meeting of cultures: Faculty and part-time doctoral students in an Ed.D. program.* Doctoral dissertation. University of Northern Iowa, Cedar Falls.

Testa, A. J. (1985). *Doctoral attrition: An exploration of role expectations of dissertation advisors and candidates in Psychology.* Doctoral dissertation, Saybrook Institute, San Francisco.

Tluczek, J. L. (1995). *Obstacles and attitudes affecting graduate persistence in completing the doctoral dissertation.* Doctoral dissertation, Wayne State University, Detroit, MI.

Wagner, D. V. (1986). *Selected personality characteristics and situational factors as correlates of completion and non-completion of the doctoral dissertation.* Doctoral dissertation, University of Michigan, Ann Arbor.

Wallace, D. D. (2000). *Critical connections: Meaningful mentoring relationships between women doctoral students and their dissertation chairpersons.* Doctoral dissertation, Louisiana State University and Agricultural and Mechanical College, Baton Rouge.

Wilkinson, C. E. (2002). *A study to determine the predictors of success in a distance doctoral program.* Doctoral dissertation, Nova Southeastern University, Fort Lauderdale, FL.

Appendix C

Assessment Instrument
for Evaluating Your Study

Herbert Simon (1957, p. 79) wrote eloquently and accurately about the limits of human reasoning. He called our limited capacity to manage an abundance of information "bounded rationality." A consequence of a limited human capacity for rationality, he observed, is that we attend to matters sequentially. Put more colloquially, we attend to the matter that shouts the loudest. In the cacophony of voices that are shouting, the dissertation may receive less than its due share of attention. The Assessment Form is intended to address this issue of under-sight by creating a structure for both assessment and interaction. Having an assessment tool helps both the doctoral advisor and the doctoral candidate, both of whom often have more obligations than can easily be met.

This instrument is designed to help the nontraditional student evaluate the proposal. It covers the basic conventional elements of the proposal, so it may lose usefulness if the researcher has elected to structure a nonconventional study. The instrument may be used by the advisor as an aid and shortcut to summarizing concerns with a proposal or dissertation draft. It may also be used as a peer assessment instrument as graduate students critique each other's work.

Assessment of Dissertation Proposals

An index at the end of this Appendix provides an interpretation of each item. A key concept associated with the assessment below is the provision for a remedy if a particular element of the dissertation proposal needs work. If there is reason to believe that an important section needs to be improved, give some thought to what remedies should be used.

Anchors

1 = Unacceptable and Remedy Required

2 = Will Require Much Reworking in Dissertation Draft; Remedy Strongly Suggested

3 = Acceptable

4 = Outstanding

1. **Dissertation Topic**

Originality	1	2	3	4
Importance	1	2	3	4

If unacceptable, proposed remedy:

2. **Purpose/Problem Statement**

Statement of Need	1	2	3	4
General Overview of Issues Surrounding Study	1	2	3	4
Clarity of Purpose of Study	1	2	3	4
Communicated Personal Interest	1	2	3	4
Persuasiveness of Language	1	2	3	4

If unacceptable, proposed remedy:

3. **Background or Context of Study**

Place of Topic in Larger Context of Practice	1	2	3	4
Quality of Analysis of Context	1	2	3	4
Identification of Key Issues	1	2	3	4
Evidence Used to Support Need	1	2	3	4
Inclusion of Major Research Findings	1	2	3	4

If unacceptable, proposed remedy:

4. **Theoretical Perspective**

Use of Theoretical Perspective	1	2	3	4
Linkage of Theory With Research Purpose	1	2	3	4

Acceptability of Atheoretical Study   1   2   3   4
If unacceptable, proposed remedy:

5. **Research Questions**
   Clarity of Question(s)   1   2   3   4
   Specificity of Question(s)   1   2   3   4
   Match With Intended Methodology   1   2   3   4
   Promise for Leading to   1   2   3   4
      New Knowledge
   If unacceptable, proposed remedy:

6. **Significance**
   Quality of the Argument   1   2   3   4
      for Significance
   Probability of Acceptance   1   2   3   4
      at Conferences
   Probability of Acceptance in Journals   1   2   3   4
   Probability of Practitioner Interest   1   2   3   4
   If unacceptable, proposed remedy:

7. **Literature Review**
   If excluded from proposal or dissertation- indicate rationale for excluding:

   If included, consideration of the following:
   Organization of the Review   1   2   3   4
   Clear Overview of Literature Presented   1   2   3   4
   Quality of Review of Research   1   2   3   4
   Scope of the Review   1   2   3   4
   Inclusion of Dissertation Studies   1   2   3   4
   Summary of Literature Review   1   2   3   4
   If unacceptable, proposed remedy:

8. **Methodology**
   Match of Method With   1   2   3   4
      Research Question
   Identification of Appropriate Subjects   1   2   3   4
   Clarity of Design   1   2   3   4
   Likelihood of Gathering Good   1   2   3   4
      Data and Information

If Quantitative

Quality of Data-Collecting Plan	1	2	3	4
Quality of Instrumentation if Appropriate	1	2	3	4
Clear Outline of Analytical Procedures	1	2	3	4
Clear Identification of Dependent Variables	1	2	3	4
Clear Identification of Independent Variables	1	2	3	4
Parameters for Determining Significance	1	2	3	4
Analysis of Potential Design Flaws	1	2	3	4

If Qualitative

Provision for Entering Field	1	2	3	4
Strategies for Interviewing if Appropriate	1	2	3	4
Strategies for Gathering Data	1	2	3	4
Strategies for Storing Data	1	2	3	4
Strategies for Analyzing Data	1	2	3	4
Strategies for Interpreting Data	1	2	3	4
Strategies for Preventing Bias	1	2	3	4
Analysis of Potential Design Flaws	1	2	3	4

9. Compliance With IRB Regulations

Application Complete	1	2	3	4

10. Mechanics of Writing

Sentence Structure	1	2	3	4
Paragraph Structure	1	2	3	4
Clarity	1	2	3	4
Overall Mechanics	1	2	3	4

If unacceptable, proposed remedy:

11. Style of Writing

Quality of Opening Rhetoric	1	2	3	4
Parsimony of Language	1	2	3	4
Flow and Logical Structure	1	2	3	4
Use of APA (or other approved style manual)	1	2	3	4
Overall Quality of Writing	1	2	3	4

If unacceptable, proposed remedy:

Definitions of Dissertation Terms

Dissertation Topic

Originality: Conventional wisdom holds that dissertations should be original work. They should be research studies (gathering of new data or preexisting data or information) that bring new knowledge or understanding to a topic. One of the best ways to know if your study is original is to read widely about your general topic.

Importance: Not all studies are of great importance, nor should they be. However, the researcher should have some claim that the findings of this study may be of importance in some small way toward advancing knowledge.

Purpose/Problem Statement

Statement of Need: In this section, the researcher should state the rationale for the study.

General Overview of Issues Surrounding Study: In this section, one should identify the issues in education that are related to the study. Few studies in education are unconnected with problems or issues of practice. One would not want to conduct a study that had no relevance or relationship to the various parts of the educational sector.

Clarity of Purpose: Dissertation researchers have an obligation to be so clear about the objectives of their study that they can discuss it with lay individuals.

Communicated Personal Interest: Dissertation writers need to communicate at least a modicum of excitement about their work. This enthusiasm for the project should be conveyed as the writer writes about the perceived importance of the work.

Persuasiveness of Language: Language is important. The study is introduced in this opening section. It is important that the language be compelling.

Background or Context of the Study

Place of Topic in Larger Context of Practice: Most research studies are inspired by inquisitiveness about a problem or theory or issue. Such studies thus have a context or a background. This section may be short but it should be present in some form.

Quality of Analysis: Familiarity with what is going on should be demonstrated. This includes information about more than the researcher's particular geographical location.

Identification of Key Issues: This section should identify those ideas or events or issues that are important.

Evidence Used to Support Need: The researcher should present some evidence that there is a need for the study, that it has the promise of doing some good in the world.

Inclusion of Major Research Findings: This is a good section in which to note just a few of the important research works that have been done on your topic.

Theoretical Perspective

Use of Theoretical Perspective: Classic quantitative studies are almost always grounded in a theoretical perspective. Using quantitative methodology, such studies seek to expand a theoretical understanding or perhaps refute it. Qualitative studies frequently do not begin with a theoretical perspective to test or examine but often utilize theory as a heuristic device to examine and interpret qualitative data. Some studies are primarily descriptive in nature and do not use theory. Some are labeled exploratory and do not use theory. However, most educational issues and problems do have theoretical explanations and the doctoral candidate is wise to consider these. For that reason, the study should be assessed in terms of its use of a theoretical perspective.

Linkage of Theory With Research Purpose: Most studies in education intend to draw some conclusion about practice. Most of those conclusions will relate in one way or another to theory that has been developed to explain behavior and practice. There should be a connection between these theoretical constructions and the research question.

Acceptability of an Atheoretical Study: Some studies intentionally avoid a theoretical grounding. If so, there should be a clear explanation as to why this is necessary, desirable, or both.

Research Questions

Clarity of Question(s): Are the questions straightforward and easily understood?

Specificity of Question(s): Research questions need to be very focused and very clear. They are guides to what the researcher does. If they are confusing, the research will end up being confused.

Match With Intended Methodology: The research question determines the methodology, not the other way around. The two must be compatible.

Promise for Leading to New Knowledge: The answers to the research question(s) should tell us things we do not know. If we already know the answers, the research questions are not the right questions.

Significance

Quality of Argument for Significance: Who will care? Why will they care? Under what conditions will they care?

Probability of Acceptance at Conferences: Dissertation research is often presented at national and regional conferences. Will this study have that potential?

Probability of Acceptance in Journals: Dissertation research is often published in academic or professional journals. Does this study have that potential?

Probability of Practitioner Interest: Will practitioners likely have any interest in the results of this study?

Literature Review

If Excluded From Proposal: Some students elect to exclude a formal literature review from their study. If so, there should be a rationale for so doing. In addition, there should be some plan for demonstrating knowledge of work in the field.

Organization of the Review: The organization of the review of research should be clearly stated at the beginning of the review.

Scope of the Review: The review of research should ground the study in the larger body of research and should be comprehensive in nature.

Inclusion of Dissertation Studies: All dissertation research should acknowledge and identify other dissertation studies on closely related topics.

Summary of Literature Review: The literature review should contain a summary, drawing all of its component pieces together.

Methodology

Match of Method With Research Question: The method must have the capacity to answer the research questions.

Identification of Appropriate Sources for Data: The method must identify the appropriate subjects or data sources to get necessary data.

Clarity of Design: The steps in the methodology should be logically and clearly laid out.

Likelihood of Gathering Good Data and Information: The methodology should be evaluated in terms of its capacity to produce useful information.

If Quantitative

Quality of Data-Collecting Plan: Data sources, whether they are people or data files, need to be available to the researcher in a timely way and need to be expected to provide accurate data.

Quality of Instrumentation if Appropriate: Surveys or attitudinal instruments need to be carefully evaluated for validity and reliability.

Clear Outline of Analytical Procedures: The statistical tools that will be used need to be appropriate for the data being gathered and appropriate to answer the research questions posed.

Parameters for Determining Significance: The researcher should specify in advance the conditions under which a significant finding will be achieved.

Analysis of Potential Design Flaws: All quantitative studies have design flaws. These should be identified.

If Qualitative

Provision for Entering Field: How one gains entrance into a qualitative environment where trust and access are critical in data collection should be discussed.

Strategies for Interviewing if Appropriate: Getting qualitative participants to speak openly and cogently is always difficult. The researcher should have a process for gathering the best qualitative data from human subjects.

Strategies for Gathering Data: Observation, interviews, videos, photography, and artifacts are all possible. Qualitative studies usually rely on multiple data sources. Are these specified?

Strategies for Storing Data: Securely storing large quantities of qualitative data is problematic. How will this be done, and are the data stored in a way that will facilitate access by the researcher?

Strategies for Analyzing Data: What approaches will the researcher take to analyze the qualitative data?

Strategies for Interpreting Data: Are there any particular ideas that the researcher has to assist in interpreting subjective data.

Strategies for Preventing Bias: Qualitative studies are highly vulnerable to researcher bias. How is this potential for bias anticipated?

Analysis of Potential Design Flaws: All qualitative studies have design flaws. These should be identified.

Mechanics of Writing

The mechanics of correct English usage are critical. The items identified on the assessment instrument are but a few of the many rules of usage. These are listed because dissertation writers so often fall prey to misuse in these areas.

Style of Writing

Quality of Opening Rhetoric: The beginnings of any journey are important. How well phrased are the introductory passages of the study?

Parsimony of Language: The language of research studies should be concise and clear. Does the study avoid excessive wordiness?

Flow and Logical Structure: The flow of sentence into paragraph, paragraph into sections, sections into chapters, and chapters into a book should be like the current of a stream. Remember that when a person is trapped in eddies, he or she can keep going around in circles. This is to be avoided in the writing of dissertations.

Use of APA (or other approved style manual): The style manual of the American Psychological Association is commonly used in education dissertations. The writer should be familiar with either this manual or another accepted manual.

Appendix D

Activities for Dissertation Support Groups

1. Identify each member of your support group. Share phone numbers, addresses, and e-mail.

2. Introduce yourself to the other members of your group. If possible, have each individual create a Web site with biographical information and pictures. Some university programs will provide space on their servers for such personal Web sites. Include a summary of your dissertation idea.

3. Discuss how you all wish to communicate (by phone conference, video conference, e-mail, chat room, in person if proximity permits, etc.). Make sure that everyone in the group is comfortable with the choice. Include in this session a discussion of how you think you want to operate in terms of organizing the group, running virtual meetings, and participating as members of the group. Give some thought to how one is supposed to be responsible to the group.

4. Have a support group virtual meeting to introduce your dissertation topic. In turns, discuss your topic and why you think it is of interest. Or, if you are close enough to do this face to face, do so. You will be impressed with how much you can gain by this type of interaction.

5. Create access to your library:
   a. All members of the group should attempt to log into their research library from home (or work, if that is where their

access is located). Read the section on using the research library and then create your access to electronic databases provided by your library.

   b. Search three databases using key words associated with your topic.

   c. Have a group conversation by phone, e-mail, or chat room about the difficulties you experienced and what you found out about your topic.

6. Search *Dissertation Abstracts* using the same key words or new key words. Report on your findings to the group. Discuss whether your key words might be expanded.

7. Spend two weeks reading. At the end of that time, have a virtual meeting and report on what you have learned. As part of this meeting, revisit the norms and operating rules you proposed for yourselves earlier. Do these make sense now that you have interacted on a number of occasions?

8. Begin to construct your introductory chapter. Begin with a problem statement and a context or background statement. You might write 15–20 pages or just a few pages. Make this the topic of a virtual group meeting.

9. Schedule a series of virtual or face-to-face meetings.

10. Make sure each member has a chance to have his or her purpose statement discussed.

11. Make sure each member has a chance to have his or her research questions discussed.

12. Begin to share drafts of Chapter One. Exchange these drafts as file attachments to e-mails.

13. At the point where a member has his or her study proposal ready, provide the means for the person to present the proposal as if doing so to the supervisory committee.

14. Celebrate each other's success.

15. Discuss how you will continue to support each other in the later stages of the dissertation writing.

As a note to this aid to working on your dissertation, do a search of the Web for dissertation support groups. You will find others who have found this type of group to be helpful.

References

Adler, M., & van Doren, C. (1940/72). *How to read a book.* New York: Simon & Schuster.

Asay, S. (1998). *Family strengths in Romania.* Doctoral dissertation, University of Nebraska—Lincoln.

Bean, J. P. (1980). Dropouts and turnover: The synthesis and test of a causal model of student attrition. *Research in Higher Education, 12,* 155–187.

Behar, R. (1996). *The vulnerable observer: Anthropology that breaks your heart.* Boston: Beacon.

Berelson, B. (1960). *Graduate education in the United States.* New York: McGraw-Hill.

Bleich, M. (1997). *After the unexpected departure of a chief nursing officer: How nurses experienced leadership transition in an acute care hospital (executive turnover).* Doctoral dissertation, University of Nebraska—Lincoln.

Bronfenbrenner, K., & Juravich, T. (2001, January 19). Universities should cease hostilities with unions. *The Chronicle of Higher Education.*

Bryant, M. Unpublished Poems. Lincoln, NE.

Bryant, M., McLellan, K., & West, J. (2002, April 22). *Beware the Jabberwocky: School district data and school assessment.* Paper presented at the meeting of the American Educational Research Association, Chicago.

Bundy, A. (1998). *Information literacy: The key competency for the 21st century.* Retrieved July 3, 2003 from www.library.unisa.edu.au/papers/inlit21. htm. (ERIC Document Reproduction Service No.ED434662).

Burbach, M. (2002). *Emotional intelligence and chair leadership behaviors.* Unpublished proposal draft, University of Nebraska—Lincoln.

Burkhart-Kriesel, C. (1992). *Social interaction in adult distance education.* Unpublished doctoral dissertation, University of Nebraska—Lincoln.

Buss, D. (2001). *Understanding freshmen student experiences living in a residential hall learning community.* Unpublished dissertation proposal, University of Nebraska—Lincoln.

Campbell, D., & Stanley, J. (1966). Experimental and quasi-experimental designs for research. In N. L. Gage (Ed.), *Handbook of research on teaching* (pp. 1–76). Chicago: Rand McNally.

Cantrell, L. (1992). *Cultural conflict among Native American and Australian Aboriginal students in mainstream universities.* Doctoral dissertation, University of Nebraska—Lincoln.

Collins, R. (1998). *The sociology of philosophies: A global theory of intellectual change.* Cambridge, MA: Harvard University Press.

Creswell, J. (1994). *Research design: Qualitative and quantitative approaches.* Thousand Oaks, CA: Sage.

Creswell, J. (1998). *Qualitative inquiry and research design: Choosing among five traditions.* Thousand Oaks, CA: Sage.

Cuban, L. (1974). *School chiefs under fire: A study of three big-city school superintendents.* Doctoral dissertation, Stanford University, Stanford, CA.

Daumal, R. (1971). *Mount analogue.* San Francisco: City Lights Books.

DiPietro, R. (2002). *The effectiveness of managerial training in a fast food restaurant chain.* Unpublished dissertation proposal, University of Nebraska—Lincoln.

Eckstrom, B. (2000). *The history of the Ronald McNair Project at the University of Nebraska.* Unpublished dissertation proposal, University of Nebraska—Lincoln.

Eisner, E. (1991). *The enlightened eye.* New York: Macmillan.

English, F. (2002). Cutting the Gordian knot of educational administration: The theory-practice gap. *UCEA Review 44,* 1–3.

Fetterman, D. (1989). *Ethnography step by step.* Newbury Park, CA: Sage.

Fitzhenry, R. (1993). *The Harper book of quotations* (3rd ed.). New York: Harper Perennial.

Fitzpatrick, J., Secrist, J., & Wright, D. (1998). *Secrets for a successful dissertation.* Thousand Oaks, CA: Sage.

Fitzpatrick, J. J. (1996). *Women mentoring women: A phenomenological study.* Doctoral dissertation, University of San Diego, San Diego, CA.

Fowler, F. Jr. (1988). *Survey research methods.* Newbury Park, CA: Sage.

Frost, R. (1969). The white-tailed hornet. In *The poetry of Robert Frost.* New York: Holt, Rinehart and Winston.

Gage, N. (Ed.). (1966). *Handbook of research on teaching.* Chicago: Rand McNally.

Gilligan, C. (1982). *In a different voice: Psychological theory and women's development.* Cambridge, MA: Harvard University Press.

Gladwell, M. (2002, December 2). Groupthink: What does Saturday Night Live have in common with German philosophy? *The New Yorker Magazine,* 102–107.

Glatthorn, A. (2002). *Publish or perish: The educator's imperative.* Thousand Oaks, CA: Corwin.

Golde, C. (1994). *Student descriptions of the doctoral student attrition process.* Paper presented at the annual meeting of the Association for the Study of Higher Education, Tucson, AZ. (ERIC Document Reproduction Service No. ED375733)

Golde, C. (1996). How departmental contextual factors shape doctoral student attrition. *Dissertation Abstracts International, 57,* 08A.

Golde, C. (1998). Beginning graduate school: Explaining first year doctoral attrition. In M. S. Anderson (Ed.), *The experience of being in graduate school: An exploration.* San Francisco: Jossey-Bass.

Golde, C. (2000). Should I stay or go? Student descriptions of the doctoral attrition process. *Review of Higher Education, 23*(2), 199–227.

Guenzel, R. (1993). *The impact of competition for grades in public schools.* Master's thesis, University of Nebraska—Lincoln.

Hamilton, A. (2002). *International non-engineering aviation doctorate curricula design for pilots: A Delphi study in a global context.* Unpublished dissertation proposal, University of Nebraska—Lincoln.

Hawkins, P. (2000). *Entry level competence of nurses by type of program.* Doctoral dissertation, University of Nebraska—Lincoln.

Heaton, R. (1994). *Creating and studying a practice of teaching elementary mathematics for understanding* (Vols. I, II). Unpublished doctoral dissertation, Michigan State University, East Lansing.

Houseman, G. (1931). Terrence this is stupid stuff. *A Shropshire lad.* New York: Henry Holt.

Jacobson, T., & Cohen, L. (2003). Evaluating Internet resources. Retrieved March 19, 2003, from http://library.edu/internet/evaluate.html

Kember, D. (1981). Some factors affecting attrition and performance in a distance education course at the University of Papua and New Guinea. *Papua New Guinean Journal of Education, 18,* 79–87.

Kember, D. (1989). A longitudinal process model of drop-out from distance education. *Journal of Higher Education, 60*(3), 278–301.

Kember, D., Murphy, D., Siaw, I., & Yuen, K. S. (1991). Towards a causal model of student progress in distance education. *American Journal of Distance Education, 5*(2), 3–15.

Knudson, T. (1997). *A grounded theory study of organizational involvement of African American and Latino students at an urban mid-western university.* Unpublished dissertation proposal, University of Nebraska—Lincoln.

Kohn, A. (1999). *Punished by rewards.* New York: Houghton Mifflin.

Land, D. (2002). Local school boards under review: Their role and effectiveness in relation to students' academic achievement. *Review of Educational Research, 71,* 229–278.

Marshall, C., & Rossman, G. (1989). *Designing qualitative research.* Newbury Park, CA: Sage.

McLellan, K. (2002). *School district variables and their contribution to student achievement.* Doctoral dissertation, University of Nebraska—Lincoln.

Merrian, S. B. (1998). *Qualitative research and case study applications in education: Revised and expanded from case study research in education.* San Francisco: Jossey-Bass.

Miller, M. (1991). *The personal motivation of chief academic development officers.* Doctoral dissertation, University of Nebraska—Lincoln.

Piantanida, M., & Garman, N. (1999). *The qualitative dissertation.* Thousand Oaks, CA: Corwin.

Plake, B. S., Impara, J. C., & Spies, R. A. (2003). *The fifteenth mental measurements yearbook.* Lincoln, NE: Buros Institute.

Publication Manual of the American Psychological Association (5th ed.). (2001). Washington, DC: American Psychological Association.

Rawlings, J. K. (1942). *Cross Creek cookbook.* New York: Charles Scribner's Sons.

Redhead, J. (2002, Spring). *Black Diamond mountaineering catalogue.* Salt Lake City, UT: Black Diamond.

Rosenthal, R., & Jacobson, L. (1968). *Pygmalion in the classroom.* New York: Rinehart.

Rossman, G., & Rallis, S. (1998). *Learning in the field: An introduction to qualitative research.* Thousand Oaks, CA: Sage.

Rossman, M. (2002). *Negotiating graduate school.* Thousand Oaks, CA: Sage.

Rothblatt, S., & Wittrock, B. (1981). *The European and American university since 1800.* New York: Cambridge University Press.

Rudestam, K., & Newton, R. (1992). *Surviving your dissertation: A comprehensive guide to content and process.* Newbury Park, CA: Sage.

Shaughnessy, A. (2001). *Early childhood educators' familiarity with oral language development.* Unpublished dissertation proposal, University of Nebraska—Lincoln.

Simon, H. (1957). *Administrative behavior* (2nd ed., p. 79). New York: Macmillan.

Son, J. A. (2000). *The impact of Confucianism on Korean principals' leadership styles and job satisfaction.* Doctoral dissertation, University of Nebraska—Lincoln.

Sookram, K. (1992). *Adult learner perceptions of issues related to the college reentry experience: A case study.* Doctoral dissertation, University of Nebraska—Lincoln.

Stattelman, W. (1999). *Parent perceptions of teacher communication.* Doctoral dissertation, University of Nebraska—Lincoln.

Strunk, W., & White, E.B. (1959). *The elements of style.* New York: Macmillan.

Thurber, J. (1956). *Further fables for our time.* New York: Simon & Schuster.

Thurston, L. (1928). Attitudes can be measured. *American Journal of Sociology, 33*(4), 529–554.

Tinto, V. (1993). *Leaving college: Rethinking the causes and cures of student attrition.* Chicago: University of Chicago Press.

Tyack, D. (1974). *The one best system.* Cambridge, MA: Harvard University Press.

Voelker, M. (2001). *Teacher to student relationships of homeless children in America's schools: How one school addressed the challenge.* Unpublished dissertation proposal, University of Nebraska—Lincoln.

Watson, C. (1971). *Father fox's pennyrhymes.* New York: HarperCollins.

Wax, M., Wax, R., & Dumont, R. (with the assistance of R. Holyrock & G. Onefeather). (1989). *Formal education in an American Indian community: Peer society and the failure of minority education.* Prospect Heights, IL: Waveland.

West, J. (2002). *School district variables and their contribution to student achievement in Nebraska Class Three public school districts.* Doctoral dissertation, University of Nebraska—Lincoln.

Wolcott, H. F. (1990). *Writing up qualitative research.* Newbury Park, CA: Sage.

Wolcott, H. F. (1995). *The art of fieldwork.* Walnut Creek, CA: AltaMira.

Wunder, S. (1994). *High school teachers' and college instructors' views of preparedness for learning United States history.* Doctoral dissertation, University of Nebraska—Lincoln.

Zinsser, W. (1990). *On writing well* (4th ed.). New York: HarperCollins.

Index